How to Raise a Rhino

DEB ARONSON

THANK YOU FOR SUPPORTING
RHINO RESCUES!

[signature]

Kuokoa Kifaru Mweusi
(Save the Black Rhino)

HOW TO RAISE A RHINO

WWW.DEBARONSON.COM

How to Raise a Rhino

a Rhino

Deb Aronson

A Dragonfeather Book
Bedazzled Ink Publishing Company * Fairfield, California

978-1-960373-04-5 paperback

Cover Photo
by
Boyd Norton

Cover Design
by

Cover Photo: Copyright Boyd Norton; all rights reserved.
Website: https://boydnorton.photoshelter.com/

Dragonfeather Books
a division of
Bedazzled Ink Publishing Company
Fairfield, California
http://www.bedazzledink.com

To my late grandmother, Charlotte Ferguson Aronson, who showed me that to travel is to live and who shared many adventures with me.

And to my late mother, Margaret Field Aronson, who showed me that when you see a problem that you care about, you should step up and do something to solve it.

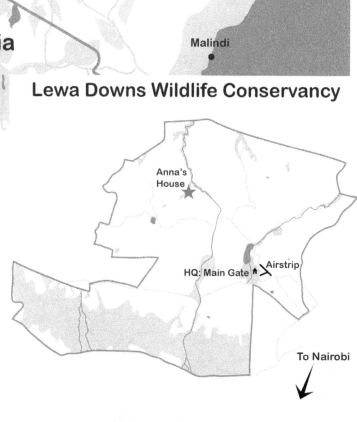

Maps by Ben Williams

Ethiopia

Kenya

Somalia

Eldoret

Lewa Downs

Kisumu

Nakuru   Mount Kenya

Garissa

Nairobi

Tanzania

Malindi

Lewa Downs Wildlife Conservancy

Anna's
House

HQ: Main Gate   Airstrip

To Nairobi

CHAPTER 1

Convoy

A slow-moving convoy drove away from the bright lights of Nairobi, toward the snowy peaks of Mt. Kenya to the north. The armed men in the lead truck held their rifles at the ready. Their eyes constantly scanned the vicinity, prepared to shoot to kill to protect their cargo. The third and last truck carried more armed men dressed in the same khaki uniforms of the Kenyan Wildlife Service (KWS). And a veterinarian.

Between them, a pickup truck carried a large wooden crate.

Wedged next to the crate sat a little, brown-haired white woman.

The woman shivered in the cold night air; she worried about the creature in the crate; she knew an attack could come at any moment. She was cold. She was anxious. She was scared.

She was ecstatic.

This was Anna Merz and the crate held her dreams. Anna had created a vast sanctuary where black rhinos could live safe from poachers. All she needed was rhinos to fill it. These first black rhinos would have babies and those babies would have babies and in this way the population of black rhinos might slowly recover.

The presence of this first, real-live rhino made her dream feel possible.

"Many people have asked me, 'why rhinos?'" she wrote. "Did I particularly like them or have a 'thing' about them? The answer is very simple: the rhinos are in Kenya and I was in Kenya, and the rhinos were in terrible trouble."

Terrible trouble indeed. An estimated 20,000 black rhinos roamed the Kenyan countryside in 1970, but by the time Anna moved there in 1980, there were only 300.

Rhino horn could fetch as much as $300,000 per horn, so poachers prowled the Kenyan countryside. These thieves murdered the rhinos, hacked off their horns, and drove off with their prize, leaving a bloody carcass and, often, an orphaned rhino infant.

Every ten minutes during the six-hour drive, Anna stood up to peer inside the crate. In the dim interior she could make out bits of rough, grey hide. Depending on how the creature turned she could see either a small eye surrounded by wrinkles or his large horn.

This enormous, powerful animal seemed surprisingly calm. He was squeaking, yes, but not bellowing or trying to shatter the crate. How funny that such an enormous creature would make such little sounds, Anna mused as she spoke to him in a soothing voice.

"As I talked to him and he squeaked back at me, it occurred to me that he was not behaving in the manner I had expected from a brainless animal; and for the first time it crossed my mind that perhaps these animals were somewhat maligned and not as stupid as everyone had assured me they were. Perhaps living with them and learning about them would be interesting after all," Anna later wrote.

CHAPTER 2

Doubt and Worry

The longer the trucks drove, the deeper the cold air dug into Anna's bones. Every two hours, when the vet stopped the convoy to check on their cargo, Anna stamped her feet, swung her arms, and worried. Physical hardship she could handle; she'd spent more than her fair share of time camping in the cold, particularly while exploring the Sahara (desert nights could be brutally cold), but she did not like feeling self-doubt.

The colder she got the more she worried. Was she a fool? What was she doing trying to save rhinos, these ugly, ill-tempered creatures? How did she think she could stop poachers? Trying to stem the tide of rhino poaching was like trying to stop a tsunami.

Beyond the problem of poachers, there were many other worries. What if she ran out of money, or they could not gather enough rhinos together to make the sanctuary work, or the rhinos didn't have any babies or all died? Plenty of people had told her it would never work. Her husband, Karl, was one of them. Was he right? Was this just "one of her wild ideas"?

Time was running out. Rhinos were vanishing quickly. She could not hesitate. People like the Craigs, who lent Anna the land for the sanctuary, and the guards they'd hired, not to mention rhinos, were counting on her. Anna shrugged to herself. All she could do was try her hardest. And that she would do.

Here she was in this truck, eye to eye with the enormous beast she was determined to save. This particular rhino kept wandering from the safety of the park in Nairobi where he lived. The wardens feared he would be killed. Ready or not, the sanctuary's first rhino was on its way.

Just before dawn, Anna saw the familiar landscape. She relaxed at the sight of the beige grasses and light-colored dirt, interspersed with the green, flat tops of umbrella acacia trees.

At last, as the rising sun lit up the countryside, they arrived at their destination, Ngare Sergoi Rhino Sanctuary. Anna saw the sign Francis (Fuzz) Dyer, her second in command, had hand painted:

NOTICE

PRIVATE. NO ENTRY WITHOUT PERMISSION

NO LIABILITY ACCEPTED FOR ANY ACCIDENTS

DO NOT LEAVE YOUR CAR

ALL RIGHTS RESERVED FOR RHINOS

She grinned and worked her arms and legs, trying to get feeling back into them. All the doubt and worry that had filled her brain on the ride up disappeared. "Wild idea" or not, they had themselves a rhino. It was time to get to work. And Anna knew how to work.

CHAPTER 3

Godot Arrives

The convoy stopped and the team transferred the big bull rhino into a large holding pen, or boma. This rhino had been named Ngotho, but Anna re-named him Godot, as in Samuel Beckett's famous play, *Waiting for Godot . . .*

In the play, the title character never shows up, but this Godot was truly here, in the flesh. *First of many, hopefully,* she thought.

Anna watched the rhino settle in. Wild animals, in particular, feel confused and scared when captured and moved. It's not like someone can explain to them what is happening. To reduce those feelings, the vet had given Godot some light tranquilizers.

But tranquilizers can make animals feel woozy; how long would it take for Godot to recover? What if Godot tried to stand and got dizzy and fell or become anxious and disoriented? Anna worried that he might hate being enclosed. He might charge the boma walls and end up injured.

Godot was so precious, Anna couldn't bear the idea that the big bull might hurt himself.

As Godot explored his enclosure in the daylight it appeared Anna's worries were unnecessary. He poked his head and large horn into all the corners. The walls, tall, straight eucalyptus poles, towered eight feet. The poles were set deep into the light brown, coarse earth, standing in two feet of concrete. The boma would keep Godot caged even if he used all his three-thousand-pound weight to charge its walls.

Anna brought Godot some alfalfa and horse nuts, a kind of horse food in pellet form. Godot had been captured and transported by crate several times in his life, so he knew about humans. But he was still a wild animal with a reputation for being mean and stupid.

Anna knew better than to let her guard down. She held out her hand. Slowly, slowly, she stretched toward the enormous creature, prepared to pull back in a blink. Godot didn't hesitate; he happily ate from her hand, his prehensile lips working like fingers to pick up each pellet and cluster of alfalfa.

Hunh, Anna thought, as she felt his lip scuff against the palm of her hand. *He is awfully well behaved for such an aggressive, mean-tempered animal.*

Anna was further amazed to find that, after a few days, she could climb right into Godot's pen. She could pick ticks off his grey, rough back. He would lean into her fingers when she scratched him at the base of his ears, almost like a cat does, so she knew he really liked that.

Ah ha, she thought, *what do the experts know about rhinos.* Look how comfortable Godot was around her. Releasing him was going to be so much easier than she imagined.

This was the first-ever rhino that any of the members of the Ngare Sergoi team had ever seen in the holding pen. Perhaps this is how all rhinos acted once captured.

Having a living, breathing rhino on the property made Anna's quest feel suddenly real. Even though one rhino was exciting, it would take many more rhinos to make any difference to the black rhinos' survival.

Anna would have to find, capture, and move a dozen or more rhinos to have enough to breed successfully. Were there that many rhinos still living in the country? And if so, where were they hiding?

Worrying about how to find more black rhinos, making sure Godot continued to thrive, and making lists of all the chores that needed to be done to get the sanctuary up and running often kept Anna awake at night.

The fencing was not finished yet, so even if they wanted to, they couldn't release Godot. Plus, they had no radios or monitoring system on the fence yet. When she thought about how much more they had to do to make the sanctuary a reality, Anna felt the way she did before she climbed a huge outcropping during her trips into the Sahara Desert. The climb was going to be exhausting. It might even push her to the edge of her abilities, but the view from the top, looking out over all creation, would be totally worth it.

Anna knew her climb had just begun, but still, here they were, with their first rhino to put on her very own reserve. Well, hers and the Craigs. It was a team effort; that she never forgot.

In six weeks, if all went well, Godot would have fully acclimated to his new home and the fence would be complete. Then they would release him to roam the entire 5,000-acre sanctuary. Godot could explore the dry, undulating hills covered in grasses, the occasional outcroppings and cliffs, the scattered acacia and fever trees, and shrubs, like the wait-a-bit bush. He could wallow in the watering holes, safe from armed poachers gunning for his horn.

CHAPTER 4

The Dodo

Anna was born on November 17, 1931, and grew up near London.

When she was very young, her father took her on day trips around the city, in part to give her mother, always in poor health, a break, and in part to spend time with Anna.

Once they wandered by display after display at the Natural History Museum in London. There, Anna caught sight of a stuffed dodo bird. She had never seen anything like this ungainly bird, with its heavy beak and short neck; so appealing in its ugliness.

Young Anna stood, mesmerized, before the display. How thrilling it would be to see a live dodo.

"No matter where you go and how hard you look, you'll never see a live dodo, because mankind hunted and killed every last one," her father said.

Anna stood rigid, her mouth open in shock as anger surged through her. She couldn't believe the greed and the cruelty. What gave these thoughtless and selfish men the right to destroy something so delightfully odd?

Anna Merz as a young girl, showing her love of animals by holding a chicken.

She carried the lesson of the dodo with her all her life. Even as an adult, when she saw an animal that needed care and protection, no matter how ungainly or ill tempered, she helped.

Decades later, when Anna saw the rhinos on the edge of extinction, her father's words came back to her. Another animal wiped off the face of the planet? Not if she could help it. She was prepared to risk her own life to help the black rhino.

Her parents loved her, but they didn't give Anna hugs or kisses or cuddles. They didn't tell her "good job, we're so proud of you," or "We love you."

When Anna was ten years old, the Germans began bombing London during World War II. It was terrifying and dangerous. Even in the midst of war, when sad and scary things happened, her parents kept a stiff upper lip, not showing or sharing emotions.

When a bomb dropped in her front yard (luckily it did not explode), or a plane crashed and burst into flame as she rode her pony, she could not go to her parents for comfort, so she hugged her dog and cried into her pony's mane.

She always felt better around animals. All her life she had at least one dog, often more, and some horses.

One day, while walking on a beach, a German fighter plane rained bullets down on her. A stranger sacrificed himself to save her, jumping between her and those bullets.

She never forgot that a total stranger died saving her life. She never forgot how fragile life could be. She never forgot the importance of helping those in need, just as she had been helped.

CHAPTER 5

Adventure

Anna had witnessed firsthand how life could be cut short with no warning. She vowed to live her life to the fullest, and, to her, that meant travel and adventure.

She did not want her parents' solid, safe middle-class life full of comfort. But her parents wanted their only child to get an education and have a career.

They found a compromise; Anna agreed to go to college and study law. Then she could travel for a year before taking the bar exam and beginning her life as a lawyer.

As soon as she graduated, in 1954, Anna went to Ceylon (now Sri Lanka), a small country off the coast of India. The two-week boat trip delivered her to a magical land so different from tweedy England that she was entranced by everything: the heat, the sight of women in their brightly colored saris, the scents of exotic spices and frangipani blooms and the practice of unusual customs, like bartering in the marketplace.

She loved it all, from the chameleon that jumped down the front of her evening dress, to losing her shoes while pushing her car out of deep mud, to seeing her first leopard, python, wild elephant, and boar.

Anna intended to return to England and keep her part of the bargain. But first, she signed up as a driver for an archaeological expedition to Pakistan where she had to drive the car over a bridge made of just two wooden planks and around hairpin turns so high she looked down upon soaring eagles.

At the Persian border (what is now Iran) the customs officials were more interested in Anna than in the items in the car. They thought the men Anna was traveling with planned to sell her in a nearby town.

"They asked (the other driver) if I was a virgin, if I could apply make-up, if I could walk in high-heeled shoes. I gathered that I would be worth two good rifles with telescopic sights if all those conditions were fulfilled. That seemed to be a fair price," Anna joked. Her sense of humor carried her through many tough times.

CHAPTER 6

Berta

Having returned from her trip to Pakistan, Anna kept her promise by taking and passing the bar exam. But just a few years later, when she was twenty-six, she visited a school friend in Kumasi, Ghana. There, she met and married her first husband, Ernie Kuhn. Their shower was a bucket suspended with a rope, their toilet was an outhouse, and their floor was dirt. Anna couldn't have been happier.

In Kumasi, Anna bred and raced horses—an ungainly white woman in a sea of black male faces—and helped Ernie run a small engineering company. Ernie made many replacement parts for cars and other machinery, an essential business in a place like sub-Saharan Africa.

As much as Anna loved adventure, she also was drawn to abandoned and exploited animals. Tending to these creatures took hours every day: injured animals needed regular doses of medicine; infants needed regular feedings.

Through her efforts she became a skilled, though amateur, veterinarian. She quickly earned the reputation for taking care of any animal brought to her. Often the animals were critically ill, having been poorly cared for or neglected.

One day a stranger delivered to Anna's house in Kumasi a package wrapped in a filthy, stinking cloth. Anna peeled back the cloth and revealed an infant chimpanzee. Upon seeing Anna, the creature screamed in terror. Anna felt like screaming too when she saw the sickly chimp. She gently cleaned it with warm water and cloths, but the chimp struggled and fought. The chimp also pooped. A lot. In less than an hour, Anna had to change her dress three times.

Frantic, Anna called her husband, Karl. *Please bring me some nappies!* she begged. By this time, she had divorced her first husband, Ernie, and married Karl Merz, another man who lived in Kumasi and worked with Ernie. In fact, he was Ernie's boss. This was the only time Anna ever put human clothes on an animal, a practice she despised.

To supplement what little the chimp could drink, Anna gave her shots of glucose and saline, to help with dehydration. In addition, the chimp, which Anna named Berta, had pneumonia and needed antibiotics. Giving any chimp shots was hard enough, but in this case, the baby was so thin and weak that the shots were agony for the little chimp.

"No wonder the poor little chimp feared me," Anna wrote.

For ten days, Anna nursed Berta. Day and night, night and day. Would Berta live? Would Berta die? Little by little, the chimp recovered. She ate with gusto. She guzzled from a bottle. One day she extended her arms to Anna: the universal request of an infant, "Pick me up!" Anna's heart lifted. Now Berta would survive, she knew.

Once Berta was strong enough, Anna would send her to the Bia reserve for orphaned chimps. There she could live a natural life with others of her kind.

The day came for Berta to leave Anna, Karl, and the dogs. What if Berta didn't thrive at the reserve? What if she got injured there? Or worse, died? Despite her worries, Anna never lost sight of her ultimate goal: for Berta to have as normal a life as possible.

Anna's friend Penny arrived to take Berta to her new home. Anna passed the chimp to her friend and could barely stand to watch as the car drove away with Berta screaming and screaming, waving her arms out the window trying to get back to Anna.

Heartsore, Anna turned away, hoping she had done the right thing.

Eight months later Anna visited the reserve and there was Berta, happy and healthy. She played with the other chimps, swinging in the trees and chattering. Berta had become a proper chimp and did not recognize Anna. Anna felt great contentment that she had saved this little life and that Berta had found a wonderful home.

Anna even tended and cared for animals she detested, like the three civet cats (a cat-like animal with a spotted coat that is related to weasels and mongoose) she named Hatred, Malice, and All Uncharitableness.

Why should an injured animal live or die based on whether she found it charming or not? She tried to give every animal in her care the best possible nursing.

When she lived in Ghana, Anna often hiked in the forest. Her favorite area was Bia, an area approximately eighty miles west-southwest of Kumasi on the border with Ivory Coast. Thanks in part to Anna's reports of the animals and plants she saw on her expeditions, this area later became the first forest national park in West Africa.

In recognition of all her work with wildlife, Anna became an honorary Ghanaian game warden. In that role, she proposed laws, some of which were enacted. The laws tried to stop people from hunting, selling, and eating wild animals, and make it illegal to own wild animals as pets.

This last law resulted in even more wild animals being dropped at her doorstep.

Anna loved seeing wild creatures up close. Once, when she was in the bush, she woke at dawn to the sound of elephants knocking down fences and tearing up gardens. Despite her fear—it's very different to be close to them in the wild than in the zoo behind a fence—she crept out of her tent and hid among the enormous roots of a massive silk cotton tree along the track the elephants took to return to the forest during the day.

She waited and waited in the misting rain. Dirku, her dog, sat close by. She wrapped her arm around him for comfort. Dirku stiffened, and the hairs on the back of Anna's neck prickled. Slowly, slowly, she looked over her shoulder.

An enormous elephant stood so close, Anna could feel its stretched out trunk just touch her like a whisper. Then, with barely a sound, the elephant walked away.

"Only the shaking dog and the elephant's tracks proved to me that I had not been dreaming," she wrote.

To be that close to that kind of wild majesty was a mystical, nearly religious experience for Anna.

CHAPTER 7

Ghana

Anna lived in Ghana for twenty years, trying to protect the forests and the animals. Her efforts did little to slow the massacre of every living thing in the Ghanaian jungle.

"Down came the forests," she wrote of her time in Ghana. "Torrential rains removed the soil. Rivers, which once ran with clear water through the forests all year, became seasonal. In the dry season they dried up and during the rainy season they became mud-filled torrents which carried the precious soil out to sea . . .

"In Ghana in front of my own eyes, I saw animal and plant species becoming extinct, and I began to realize how terribly quickly this could happen . . . Animals began to disappear from the savannah as well as the forest, and to reappear in the markets as 'bush meat.'"

When Anna asked local Ghanaians about the disappearance of animals they often shrugged and said the animals "had traveled."

At any marketplace, shoppers could find monkey pelts, leopard skins and teeth, horns of various creatures, not to mention—even more heart-breaking—live baby monkeys, birds, and other creatures taken from their mothers.

Anna tried to help where she could. She regularly rescued live creatures as they came to her attention. Happily, Ernie, her first husband, shared her love of animals and agreed with the need to rescue them when possible. His only restrictions were, "no parrots and no monkeys."

But then one day Ernie came home for lunch and suggested they have a glass of wine. This was unusual, but Anna humored him. He asked if he could borrow Anna's car to take back to work with him. He'd parked his pickup truck up the road in some shade. It had a little gift in it for Anna.

Curiosity aroused, Anna trotted up to the truck. "Inside were six long bamboo poles and attached to them by their feet were forty-six African grey parrots, all immature and all with their wings clipped," she wrote.

"Parrots, you will recall, were one of the two creatures Ernie had expressly asked me not to keep. But he had seen them in the market, hanging head down in the full sun and, unable to bear the sight, he had bought the whole lot then and there."

Half the birds died within two days, but they found homes for the rest.

When she and her second husband, Karl retired to Kenya in 1976, it was in part to get away from the depressing environmental situation in Ghana.

Anna imagined that the kind of environmental destruction she witnessed in Ghana didn't occur in Kenya. But sadly, just as in Ghana, the people of Kenya harvested every creature from the countryside in the quest to make money.

In the market, stacks of zebra or Colobus monkey hides enticed shoppers. Lion teeth and dik-dik horns were piled high in the stalls. Vendors also offered bush meat, which could be almost any kind of wild animal killed and sold for food.

Anna could not bear witness to the destruction of yet another ecosystem. She could not stand idly by while, once again, more wildlife went the way of the dodo. No one would admit to the problem. And who could blame them? The problem was so enormous there was no solution, certainly no simple solution.

There had to be a way to fight back. Anna began to imagine creating a sanctuary. A sanctuary is not a zoo, where animals are on display, but a large, protected habitat where wild animals are free to roam in safety.

She had heard an elephant expert give a lecture in Nairobi about the poaching of elephants. She thought she'd work to create an elephant sanctuary.

Her first obstacle was that non-Kenyans could only own ten acres; not enough space to save anything much bigger than a porcupine. Another problem was that Kenyan landowners who had enough acreage were not interested in devoting it to a sanctuary of any kind.

How would a sanctuary help them make a living, the farmers wanted to know? Everyone knew wild animals in Kenya were nothing but trouble, attacking and eating their livestock, uprooting their gardens, and tearing down their fences. Many of them laughed at Anna, this wacky white woman who had just moved to their country. What did she know about how things were done? Anna felt discouraged, but she did not give up. She brought up her idea everywhere she went.

Then, in 1982—six years after she and Karl moved to Kenya—they took a weeklong holiday at a safari camp called Wilderness Trails, six hours drive north of Nairobi. Here she finally found some landowners, David and Delia Craig, who were interested.

CHAPTER 8

Wilderness Trails Safari Camp

David and Delia Craig owned tens of thousands of acres of land at the foot of Mt. Kenya since the 1920s, when Delia's family had emigrated from England. The Craigs farmed and ranched in the region for several generations. They loved the land and its inhabitants, including the wild animals.

At Wilderness Trails Safari camp, visitors slept in tents and hiked, rode horses, and drove through the rolling, scrubby lands scattered with acacia trees and inhabited by elephants, giraffes, lions, leopards, and water buffalo. Anna was in heaven.

As Anna enjoyed her outings, in addition to wild animals everywhere, she saw cows and goats. The animals seemed to co-exist just fine. Perhaps the other landowners she'd spoken to didn't realize domestic and wild animals could live side by side.

Once again her dream bubbled up to the top of her mind. Perhaps . . . perhaps . . . perhaps the Craigs might be interested in her idea? But David Craig, a tall, craggy, white man, intimidated Anna. He reminded her of her own intense, remote father.

Anna stalled for days, trying to work up her courage. Would her dream falter simply because she was too timid to speak up? What did she have to lose? The worst that could happen was David would say no, just like all the other landowners she'd approached.

Anna finally got the nerve to approach the Craigs. She stammered and stuttered. She feared David and Delia thought she was talking nonsense, but to her enormous relief they were immediately intrigued. They called for their son, Ian, to join them. Anna described her vision of finding somewhere with enough land to gather endangered elephants together and enable them to breed in safety.

Photo courtesy of Lewa Wildlife Conservancy

Ian Craig, seen here in 2017, was the son of David and Delia Craig, the landowners who originally gave Anna permission to begin her sanctuary at Lewa Downs. Today, Ian heads an expansive network of sanctuaries, known under the umbrella of Northern Rangelands Trust.

The Craigs wanted to know more.

They took Anna with them to their home on a bluff overlooking the buff landscape, to continue discussing the details. Anna could hardly believe it. Could it be, after all this time, that there was a landowner who might share her vision?

Anna outlined her idea for a fenced-in elephant sanctuary. She had enough money to build the fence and hire guards, she told the Craigs.

They'd need to hire numerous guards who were well trained and prepared to protect the animals, Anna had learned. That meant being willing to shoot intruders. And the guards had to be paid well enough that they wouldn't be tempted to poach the animals themselves. From the beginning, guards were paid twice what they could earn outside the sanctuary.

The Craigs liked what they heard and offered to set aside five thousand acres of their property, which they called Lewa Downs, to support her project. In the midst of their discussion, however, David said, "Everyone's doing elephants, how about your doing rhinos?"

"But I don't know anything about rhinos," Anna said.

"You'll learn," David answered.

And so it was, Ngare Sergoi Rhino Sanctuary was born. Ngare Sergoi is the name of a nearby river. It translates from the Masai as "River of Donkeys."

Anna took David seriously and set out to learn everything she could about all species of rhinos: the black, the white, the greater one-horned, the Sumatran and the Javan. While she was unable to travel to Java or Sumatra, Anna spent six weeks in India observing the greater one-horned rhino. She traveled to South Africa to observe how they captured white rhinos and the techniques they used to reduce stressing the animals. Everywhere she went people also shared information, scientific papers and she absorbed it all.

Anna's passion very quickly became black rhinos and only black rhinos.

"Everything was rhino for Anna," Ian Craig says. "Anything that was a negative to rhino was a negative to Anna . . . she hated elephants."

The problem with elephants is that they knock over trees before eating the leaves. Black rhinos eat dozens of types of shrubs that thrive in the shade of those trees. When the trees get knocked over that destroys the shrubs black rhinos depend on.

To protect the shrubs for the rhinos, different areas of the sanctuary were fenced off internally from the elephants, but often they broke through.

Every time Anna saw elephants where they didn't belong, she tried to run them off with her little yellow Suzuki truck. But elephants are so smart they quickly recognized her distinctively colored vehicle. When they saw her coming, they uprooted trees and laid them across the road, blocking her way. Sometimes they even chased her. It got so bad, Fuzz painted Anna's truck green so it matched all the trucks on the sanctuary and the elephants would no longer be able to recognize her specific truck.

A line of elephants heading for water. Anna didn't love how the elephants tore up the trees, destroying the vegetation for black rhinos.

CHAPTER 9

Gaining Trust

Anna had the land and a name. Now she had to build the actual sanctuary. Luckily, she had inherited some money from her father and could spend the interest on that money. The interest income was enough for her to fund her dream.

The money paid for the fencing and the guards and her living expenses. Her personal needs were simple.

As Ian Craig said, "As long as she had some horses and dogs, she was happy."

Anna and Karl built themselves a small, simple house on the sanctuary. Ian's brother, Will, described it as "unremarkable; a pre-fab rectangle with a kitchen and dining room separate."

The house had a lovely verandah, which looked out over a hidden ravine that flowed with water year around. Anna loved to visit the lush stands of papyrus (marula) and the large fig tree at the bottom of the ravine.

Her compound also had a small stable for her horses (and dogs), and a guesthouse for her numerous visitors.

Karl lived with Anna on the sanctuary, but he did not contribute to the project. This was entirely Anna's baby.

Anna oversaw the installation of eight-foot-tall, electrified fencing around the five thousand acres of rolling scrubland dotted with acacia trees and shrubs. Mt. Kenya, craggy and often snow covered, loomed in the distance.

Everyone assured Anna that rhinos were big, unpredictable, and not terribly bright. Rhinos are not attractive like giraffes or majestic like elephants. Their hide is rough like tree bark, not soft, glossy, and decorative like a cheetah or leopard.

They have the reputation for being short tempered, belligerent, solitary, and stupid. Historically rhinos have been considered pests, a menace.

But Anna knew that, as belligerent and unattractive as they were, they still deserved protection. The rhino was a lot like the dodo. Not being the brightest or most attractive creature was no excuse for humans to wipe them off the face of the earth.

Anna spent eighteen months building the sanctuary and traveling to study rhinos elsewhere as wild rhinos continued to disappear.

CHAPTER 10

Hunting for Rhinos

Between the destruction of their habitat and the bandits killing them for their horns, rhinos really needed Anna's help.

Hundreds of thousands of black rhinos inhabited the area south of the Sahara Desert over a century ago. Even though black rhinos don't roam in herds like wildebeest or elephants, the high number of them made them easy to find.

The general wisdom until the 1980s could be roughly translated into "the only good rhino is a dead rhino." But attitudes changed dramatically as the rhino was hunted to near extinction.

Suddenly it became very important to save them.

But where were they?

Even in the few short years since Anna had moved to Kenya, wild black rhinos had almost disappeared. Where once she might come across one while strolling outside her neighborhood near Nairobi, the only place to see evidence of wild animals was in the market, where locals sold skins, teeth, and meat.

"They put up the fence [around the sanctuary], but then it took a long time, maybe a month, to find a rhino we could rescue," Kinyanjui said, one of the best Masai trackers at the sanctuary and a close friend of Anna's. "We looked everywhere, Samburu, Isiolo, Laikipia, Meru. We were fighting [competing] with poachers to catch survivors. At Ololokwe we knew of five rhinos but could only find one [by the time they got ready to capture and move them]."

Rhinos were certainly disappearing fast, but Anna and Ian had heard that a rhino had been spotted on Shaba reserve about forty miles northeast of Lewa. Anna thought it was worth going just to see if she could find the rhino. She couldn't capture the rhino on her own, but she felt compelled to go, just to see what she could see.

She and Thomas, one of the trackers who had been hired at the sanctuary, drove her truck for many miles over rough dirt roads and arrived at noon at a river in the reserve.

The heat was ferocious as the sun baked the land.

Anna and Thomas decided to linger by the car until the worst of the heat passed. The full moon would be bright enough to easily return to the car after dark.

Anna rested in some meager shade, eyeing the river nervously. Not so long ago she had floundered across a river in Nepal to get away from a tigress, while fearing she'd be eaten by a crocodile.

The day was so hot Anna had no appetite. But Thomas made a fire to brew Samburu tea. He filled a saucepan with cool water, tea leaves, sugar, and powdered milk and then boiled the concoction "wildly until well stewed." Anna found it surprisingly refreshing, a "most excellent drink and very sustaining."

Rejuvenated, Thomas hiked up his shorts and the red cloth he wore as a cape, and Anna clapped her tattered, white straw hat onto her head, and they waded across the river.

Thomas carried a spear as their only protection against animals and a bottle of water as protection against the heat. Every time he saw Anna's face get to a certain shade of red, he stopped and poured water over her hat and face to cool her off.

They soon found some rhino tracks in the sandy, beige dirt. Shortly after that they saw some droppings. They were dry and light brown and clearly had vegetable matter in them, but were they rhino?

Thomas fished out Anna's eyeglasses from under his cape, and Anna got down on her hands and knees to inspect the dung.

"We both knelt beside the exciting bits of dung and discussed the implications in a variety of languages," Anna wrote, finding that image amusing. Thomas did not speak much English and Anna did not speak much Swahili, the common language in Kenya. Anna could not tell if Thomas knew what kind of dung it was.

They gave up on identifying the dung and continued to follow the trail, but soon the ground became so rocky the tracks disappeared. They decided to continue in the same direction, across the plain with very little shade and toward Shaba Mountain.

As the ground grew steeper and rougher, thorny wait-a-bit acacia shrubs grabbed and tore at Anna's pants, which were soon shredded and her legs bloody. Meanwhile everywhere she looked little klipspringers—a small, native antelope—jumped about as if this were the easiest terrain to navigate.

Anna and Thomas frequently paused to catch their breath as they climbed toward the northern peak of Shaba Mountain. They finally made it to the top, and the view in the just setting sun was breathtaking. They could see for miles over the undulating land.

Much to Anna's disappointment, they didn't see any rhinos. They returned to the truck by the light of the full moon.

As they made camp, Anna could hear lions roaring and was happy Thomas had brought his spear. Thomas cooked cabbage, corned beef, and maize flour and over the fire for a hearty meal. They washed it down with more Samburu tea. They added more branches to the fire, rolled up in their blankets, and went to sleep. The stars shone brightly overhead.

All night Anna heard elephants walking by. They passed so close she could hear the rumbling of their tummies. Sometimes there were other, scarier noises. Thomas got up and threw a branch in the direction of the sound.

The next day, well before dawn, they continued their quest. They clambered over increasingly rough, rocky terrain. They toiled up a steep, dry riverbed full of rocks.

As Anna climbed over some of the rocks, she wished for a rope to help her over the steepest spots. She was surprised to find dung from large animals and realized that both elephants and rhinos navigated seemingly impassable terrain with relative ease. But how?

Despite all their climbing and searching, they never spotted a rhino. Anna didn't mind so much. She loved hiking, no matter what she saw—or didn't see—or what hardships she experienced.

CHAPTER 11

First Capture

With a rhino in residence, Anna, Ian, and Fuzz were determined to capture black rhinos from the surrounding countryside. They heard that a rhino had been sighted east of Shaba Mountain, and they spent days of planning to try and capture it.

Many people wanted to be part of the epic event, so they had to figure out how to accommodate both people and equipment. The convoy included:

- two trackers;
- a vet;
- Ian and Ian's wife, Jane;
- their two children;
- Jane's mother;
- an infant mongoose named "Goose," which had to be fed so often it couldn't be left home.
- One angry lion that had been stealing livestock in the area.

They filled four trucks plus two aircraft: Will, Ian's brother and a pilot, joined them in his red Piper Cub; as did a pilot named Ted and his helicopter.

Ian was determined, with permission from the Kenyan Wildlife Department, to release the lion on the Shaba Reserve, rather than kill it. Usually a wild animal stealing livestock would simply be shot.

Anna, in her distraction and general clumsiness, almost missed the whole show. As exciting as the big day was, chores were chores and they had to be done. So that morning, like every morning, she mucked out her horses' stalls and fed and watered them. Typically, she also went riding to exercise the horses, but she skipped that today; they had a rhino to rescue!

She could not skip the worming tablets, however. Horses often get worms in their intestines, which can make them lose weight, have low energy and gradually make them very sick. It was a routine procedure, one that took place every couple of months.

After giving the tablet to a horse, Anna felt a pinch. She looked down and saw two of her fingers gushing blood. She realized that the horse had bitten off the tops of her fingers, down to the first joint. Clearly not something she could fix with a band-aid. Karl had already headed into Nanyuki, the nearby town, so she wrapped her mangled fingers in a cloth and dashed to the clinic in town on her own. There, they dressed her fingers as well as they could and urged her to go to the next largest town to get her wound properly taken care of.

Nonsense, she said, it was just a couple fingertips. She wasn't going to miss them.

She insisted the nurses there just bandage her up as best they could. Her tetanus shot was up to date and she couldn't spare the time. She had observed rhinos in various other countries in the course of her rhino research, but she'd never participated in a capture. She would not miss it on account of a few fingertips.

Here is Anna's diary entry from that day:

> Livestock, made breakfast for K[arl] early and he went to Nanyuki [the nearby town] and I got the top of both 4th and 5th fingers on my right hand bitten off . . . Oh hell, teach me to be more careful.

CHAPTER 12

The Search

The day was so hot they put a canvas cover over the lion's cage and wetted it with water periodically. The evaporation as they drove cooled the beast and prevented it from getting heat stroke.

They got to the reserve and drove as close as they could to the river, a good place to release the lion. Ian tossed a rope over a tree branch and then tied one end of the rope to the cage's trap door and the other to his bumper.

Everyone retreated to their cars. Ian drove his truck forward, lifting the trap door. The lion gave a mighty snarl and leaped out into the lush growth on the bank of the river, never to be seen again. This first part of their mission was a quick and easy success.

The convoy then drove to where the rhino had been spotted and set up camp. They spent the next day plotting their course of action.

The basic plan was 1) dart the rhino with a tranquilizer 2) load it onto a truck 3) carry it back to a nearby boma that had been built. The main obstacle was the rhino lived in an area with high craggy cliffs surrounded by expansive plains. Where the cliffs met the plains, boulders and bushes tumbled together in a tangle, much like where Anna and Thomas had explored during their earlier, unsuccessful trip.

That meant if they darted the rhino and it ran into an area they could not access, with either the recovery drug or the truck, the rhino might die. They hoped the helicopter and plane would not only help them spot the rhino, but herd it toward a location with easy access for the truck to load its precious cargo.

Because Anna's injured hand made her even more uncoordinated than usual, her team refused to let her be part of the group on the ground. Instead she joined Will in his little red airplane.

Will took off at dawn to search the mountainside from the sky. Every so often, he turned the engine off and glided on the big, warm air currents coming off the mountainside. He loved flying like this.

Whenever Anna heard a plane fly over, she cringed; a holdover from her childhood during the war. Flying was different, however. She had only flown in a small plane once before, but she never turned away from an adventure. Besides, this was her chance to spot a rhino.

Once they were aloft, she was so focused on looking for any sign of the rhino she didn't have time to feel nervous, even when Will turned the engine off. They searched the rugged country below them until Anna's eyes dried out, but they saw no signs of the elusive rhino.

Likewise, the ground crew found nothing. Will landed the plane for a short break and then took off again. This time the helicopter also joined in the search.

For two and a half hours the two airborne teams flew a careful pattern above the treetops, back and forth across the jagged mountain. Will and Anna were in constant radio contact with the groups on the ground. At one point, Ian radioed he found tracks and had a fleeting glimpse of the rhino near a jumble of boulders and brush where the base of the mountain met the plain.

In the air Will also spotted the rhino briefly, though Anna had not. It's hard to imagine, but a large rhino can hide itself almost in plain sight. No one on the ground or in the air saw the wily rhino again in several hours of searching.

Finally, a local huntsman told Ian's group of trackers that he saw the rhino leave the mountain two hours earlier. The rhino escaped over such a rugged slope of rocks, Anna did not think even an agile klipspringer could have navigated it safely.

Who knew that rhinos could be agile and light on their feet? She was beginning to appreciate that rhinos were more complex than everyone claimed.

CHAPTER 13

Shaba

After hours of fruitless searching, everyone regrouped at the camp to figure out the next step. The local huntsman thought the rhino had gone into a thicket of tangled brush at the base of a hill. The trackers circled the thicket entirely and found no tracks. They couldn't imagine an enormous rhino sneaking into that thicket and leaving no trace.

Still.

Anna, Ian, Bob, and three trackers decided to creep into the brush just to make sure the rhino was gone. They walked with caution, crouching under branches, stepping over branches, keeping a sharp eye out for anything that might move even a centimeter in the cover of the thicket.

Soon they came upon a large pile of rhino dung so fresh the smell was overpowering.

"Be ready to jump into a tree," Ian whispered to Anna.

She nodded, knowing with her injured hand and epic clumsiness, she'd never succeed.

Out of the corner of her eye, Anna saw a dark mass move and heard a loud snort just a few steps away. Someone pushed her down behind a tree and the rhino charged right between Ian and Kinyanjui, one of the trackers, barely missing them. Bob swung up like an acrobat on a branch that stretched across the track.

Dieter, the veterinarian, darted the fleeing rhino from the helicopter that was hovering nearby and the chase was on. Ian and several other men took off running, with Anna huffing along behind. The helicopter kept the rhino in its sights, guiding the team on the ground to the rhino.

After about fifteen minutes of running, the rhino collapsed onto its side. The helicopter landed, and Dieter got off to monitor the rhino's heart rate and breathing.

Meanwhile, Ian hopped in the helicopter to go get the tractor. Anna came shambling up to the gathered group just as the helicopter lifted off with Ian inside. Luckily the rhino, a female, had gone down in an area the tractor could access.

It is important to shift an unconscious rhino on to its chest, or brisket, as soon as possible. Lying on its side for a long time can strain a rhino's heart. But together Dieter, Anna, and Kinyanjui did not have the strength to roll it. Anna stripped off her shirt, dampened it, and laid it over the rhino's eyes to protect it from the brutal sun that beat down on them.

Clad only in her bra, she dragged the rhino's head out of the dust and laid it across her knees. Everyone tried not to act surprised by Anna's actions, but it was startling. Kinyanjui also used his shirt to cover the rhino, though it didn't cause the same degree of confusion and embarrassment. Others poured water over the rhino to keep it cool, soaking Anna also.

Finally, the tractor with the sledge arrived, bumping over the rough terrain. The rhino was tied up with padded ropes. The team pushed and pulled the enormous beast onto the sledge, which was a flat, open pallet.

The tractor took the rhino away, slowly navigating the ruts and rocks, careful to not bruise their cargo. Just as with Godot, a Wildlife Department truck with armed guards led the caravan. They drove two hours over unpaved tracks to a small holding boma within the Shaba Reserve they had built for the undertaking.

The team untied the rhino and injected a recovery drug into her ear. Then Anna and Dieter watched over the rhino to make sure she regained consciousness and didn't suffer any ill effects from the tranquilizer. Anna worried the rhino had been on her side too long. Also, two hours was a long time for it to be fully sedated.

They waited and waited. Would the rhino recover? Anna's heart and stomach felt jumpy. Still no signs of recovery.

Anna and Dieter crept into the boma and sprinkled water on the rhino. The rhino wiggled her ears. She gave a snort. She lifted her head. Slowly, in the gathering dusk, she wobbled to her feet. Anna and Dieter dashed from the pen, ecstatic.

A few minutes later, the rhino stood magnificent and prehistoric, and Anna and Dieter breathed a sigh of relief and went off to join the others for dinner. An armed guard was posted to watch over the rhino at all times.

CHAPTER 14

Waiting is over . . .

Shaba, named after the area in which they found her, would stay in this holding boma, under guard, until the fencing was done.

A few weeks after they captured Shaba, the sanctuary was at last ready for rhinos. Godot could be immediately released into the sanctuary. Anna and Fuzz, Ian, and others gathered at the boma. Here was another big moment in Anna's journey.

Anna and Fuzz opened the wooden gate. They expected Godot, so docile in the boma, to simply wander off into the bush. But as the gate swung open, Godot charged out of the boma aiming for the gathered people.

Horn down, feet pounding, no longer the docile creature who stood placidly while he got scratched behind his ears, Godot was out for blood.

Without thinking, Fuzz shoved Anna up a tree and followed after her. Godot snorted. He stamped. He ran around the tree, tossing his horn. He knocked over small shrubs. When would it end?

Finally, after what felt like forever, but was likely only several minutes, Godot did wander off into the scrub to investigate his new domain.

It turned out that, outside the boma, Godot became the "meanest machine you'd ever see," Fuzz said. "You could get that animal to charge just by whistling."

Anna, on left, Fuzz Dyer in the middle and his father, Tony, to the right. Samia the infant is also pictured.

Once down from the tree, Anna dusted off her clothes and grinned at Fuzz. Giddy with having escaped disaster so early in their undertaking, she realized she still had a lot to learn.

Shortly after Godot was released into the sanctuary, Shaba arrived from the heavily guarded holding boma near where she was captured. She spent several days in the boma at the sanctuary, to allow her to adjust and recover from her travels.

With two rhinos on the property, Anna felt relief and excitement about finally doing something in the face of all the destruction and greed she'd witnessed, especially over the decades she'd lived in Ghana.

When she started, Anna could hardly imagine what she was getting into. It turns out, for example, she learned that not all black rhinos are the same. Remembering how docile

Godot was in the boma, she expected the same from Shaba. But Shaba treated the boma like a prison, not a spa, as Godot had.

Every morning Anna carried armfuls of lucerne, or alfalfa, to Shaba. Like a red cape in front of a bull, Anna's arrival was Shaba's signal to charge the walls of the boma, head down, heels flying, snorting angrily. Anna struggled to keep her voice calm and not leap away as the roaring rhino charged

Each time Shaba stopped just before she rammed into the tall, strong eucalyptus fencing, dust and small pebbles flying in every direction. Even if Shaba knew enough to not actually collide with the walls of the boma, clearly she was feeling highly stressed and that could not be healthy.

Day after day, Anna visited the boma. She spoke to Shaba in a calm voice: *don't worry, we're here to help you, don't be scared.* She offered Shaba lucerne and horse nuts. She spent time near Shaba, hoping the rhino would eventually get used to her.

It's not that Anna wanted the rhinos to be so comfortable around humans that they were like pets, but she hoped Shaba would stop freaking out every time she brought her food. Often, time and proximity eventually acclimated a creature to humans, Anna knew. She just had to figure out how to calm this wild rhino down.

Anna had a lot of tricks up her sleeve when trying to earn an animal's trust. Once, when she lived in Ghana, a man led a dog into her yard on a long rope. No one, not even the dog's owner could get close to the creature, he said.

Although the dog had the jackal face of a bush dog, she also had lovely dark spots like a Dalmatian. Anna bought her, she claimed, because the dog reminded her of her beloved dog Pudding, a dog she'd had in England that had come with her to Ghana.

Besides, Anna believed with all her being that if she truly felt and showed deep love and compassion she could win the trust of most any animal.

Anna kept the dog, which she named Linda, on a long rope, and attached the other end of the rope to her waist when she was home. That meant the dog had to follow her around, though always at a distance. She never approached the dog. She knew not to force the relationship. Linda had to come to her.

As Anna went about her chores, she spoke quietly and soothingly to the dog. Usually she would narrate what she was doing. *Now I'm going to boil some water for tea. A cup of tea would taste lovely this afternoon,* she might say in her calmest voice as the dog followed her on the rope.

This went on, hour after hour and day after day. Then, one day, after about two weeks, Anna sat reading in the garden and the dog sidled up to her.

"She crept up and put her nose on my leg," Anna told Ernie that night at dinner. "I talked to her and then suddenly she was on my lap with her head pressed against me, quivering and crying out the story of her troubles. I held her and took the rope off."

Anna thought perhaps reading might calm Shaba. She climbed up to a platform above Shaba's head and opened *Collected Works of William Shakespeare*. Every day she would bring lucerne and read for two hours to Shaba. The rhino stopped charging. Anna kept reading. Finally, one day, Shaba ate alfalfa from Anna's hands, her prehensile lips scuffing Anna's hand just as Godot's had.

CHAPTER 15

Shaba and Morani

Ironically, when Shaba was finally released to roam the sanctuary, she presented a new and unexpected problem. Even when the gate of the holding boma swung open, Shaba wouldn't leave. Her prison had become her refuge.

Shaba hung around, making it almost impossible for Anna and the others to get to their car and go home. The next morning Anna returned, and found Shaba, back in her boma and making little squeaks as if to say, "Feed me!" Anna lured her out with alfalfa and then slammed shut the gate. Eventually Shaba got the message and wandered off.

While Anna was trying to settle Shaba down in the boma, a third rhino arrived at the sanctuary. Like Godot, this next rhino—Morani—was delivered from a nature park. And, like both Godot and Shaba, Morani's behavior and personality was full of surprises.

Morani, which means "warrior" in Swahili, had been born at the Amboseli National Park, south of Nairobi. When he was less than a year old, poachers murdered his mother to steal her horn. Sadly, even rhinos in sanctuaries are not entirely safe from these bandits.

Morani needed help. He could not survive on his own. Typically baby rhinos live with their mothers for at least three years before they can fend for themselves. Sometimes males stay with their moms even longer because older, bigger males attack them.

Because Morani was so young when his mother died, he was originally moved to an animal orphanage near Nairobi where a team of trained caretakers raised him. After he'd grown bigger, he returned to Amboseli. Even though Morani was on the small side and a pacifist, (like *Ferdinand the Bull* in the children's book by Munro Leaf), a jealous bull rhino, who did not like the presence of another male in his territory, threatened and harassed him.

Every time Morani felt unsafe, he took refuge by sneaking into the bar of one of the resort's lodges. Imagine being on safari and going into the bar to get something to drink and coming face to face with a male rhino, horn and all.

Morani obviously couldn't continue to live in the wild at Amboseli.

So six-year-old Morani found himself in a traveling crate headed up the highway to Ngare Sergoi. He arrived at the sanctuary shortly after Shaba and was placed in a boma right next to Shaba's.

Morani saw Shaba and perked right up. He followed her every move. He tried to communicate with her through the walls of the boma, using various huffing and breathing patterns Anna would eventually come to recognize as rhino-speak.

Once released from the boma and given the opportunity to roam the entire sanctuary, Morani only rarely left Shaba's side. Typically male and female rhinos who are mating do not spend a lot of time together, but Morani stayed with Shaba almost constantly. Morani's behavior was more like that of a rhino calf with a mother rhino. Perhaps she was a mother figure for him, replacing the mother he had lost as an infant.

Morani was a peaceful, mellow rhino. He got along with all the animals on the sanctuary, even the cattle, which often engulfed him within the herd, wandering all around him. Sometimes Anna saw calves licking his back legs while Morani calmly browsed.

For some reason known only to himself, the only animal he didn't get along with were donkeys. Anna occasionally spotted him chasing a donkey or two down the dirt road.

Like Ferdinand the Bull, Morani loved lying in the sun. His daily patterns were very regular, which made him easy to find. He mostly stayed in a small area just south of Anna's house.

Unlike other rhinos who rested in the shade of a tree and were surprisingly hard to spot, Morani liked to lie out in an abandoned cattle boma. Not only was he easy to spot, he also felt very comfortable around humans, so when visitors came wanting to see a black rhino, Morani was often Anna's first choice.

CHAPTER 16

More Rhinos

Morani may have been sweet natured, but he also was curious, and this created a new challenge for Anna and the others. About a month after Morani was released to roam across the enclosed land, three more rhinos were delivered to Ngare Sergoi.

These three rhinos had been captured by the Kenyan Wildlife Service (KWS) in an area to the west of Mt Kenya and southwest of Ngare Sergoi. Anna and Karl used to hike in that area in the early 1980s and they often saw rhino tracks. They sometimes got close enough to even hear them. But in 1983 poachers moved in and decimated the population. Only these three rhinos remained. KWS brought the three rhinos to Ngare Sergoi, where they could live in relative safety.

The KWS named two of the rhinos Rongai and Amboni. Those rhinos arrived at the sanctuary first. Rongai was a large female and Amboni, who Anna thought might be her son, was a small, young male.

A big group of people, including several members of Ian Craig's family, came to the boma to witness the arrival of the two rhinos, which were being transferred from their travel crate to the holding boma. Amboni was half out of the travel crate, and Morani appeared.

"Morani's great head came peeping round the corner of the boma with an expression totally comic with curiosity," Anna wrote. "Total consternation all around and everybody, at least 40 of them, lept [sic] over everything. Me up the ladder, Morani slowly came towards this incredible scene and first fell over the poles, then backed into the Toyota.

"Everyone laughed and then he dug furiously in the dust which showered in all direction, then he tried his hand at tipping over the long crate [that Amboni was in], rhino and all, but was very huffy . . . Eventually he moved to a reasonable distance and allowed us to proceed with unloading our new pair."

After one week, during which Amboni and Rongai became acclimated to their new home, it was time to release them from the boma. Near dawn, Anna came out of her house and there was Shaba, hanging around her fence.

Shaba, as terribly behaved as she was in the boma, had become intrigued by or attached to humans, or at least to Anna, and was a bit of a pest. But at least, when Anna waved her flashlight and yelled "shoo shoo," Shaba "shoo'd."

Anna had not slept well the previous night. Roaring lions had kept her awake. Worrying about how long her money would last also kept her from sleeping.

Still, captive animals, domestic or otherwise, don't care if you are tired or not, you still have to take care of them. Anna fed her livestock, tended to Rongai and Amboni, rode her horses, did household chores, and went "rhinoing" as she called it, with one of the trackers. She was very happy to see Godot on a far hill, looking settled in. Just a routine day for Anna.

That afternoon Anna went to release Rongai and Amboni. Releasing rhinos into the sanctuary never got old. Every time the boma gate swung open and a rhino left to wander the sanctuary, whether they charged out or wandered out, Anna had a momentous feeling that she and her team were doing something concrete and productive to help save an entire species from extinction.

Anna opened Rongai's gate first, and she sauntered out without a hitch. Amboni appeared quite nervous. Perhaps he was remembering the excitement when Morani tried to tip his crate during his arrival. Eventually he, too, headed off.

The next morning Anna woke up very early. She was curious where Amboni went and how he was doing, so she took a drive. She came upon him near headquarters. Amboni awoke at the sound of her car and chased her. Luckily for Anna, he got mixed up in a herd of giraffe.

Amboni was not going to be a rhino Anna could approach safely. It was a good reminder that the rhinos, no matter how close she grew to them, no matter how many she observed, and no matter how much she learned, were wild creatures capable of great destruction.

That same day the last of the three rhinos from the plateau area arrived from the KWS. Anna christened this last rhino Kelele ("noise" in Swahili) because he made so much noise. But, unlike Shaba, he ate out of Anna's hand from the very beginning. Even though he didn't need calming down like Shaba had, Anna discovered she enjoyed reading to the rhinos, and so she read to him about owls. Perhaps it was this poem, which she wrote out in her journal:

> A wise old owl sat in a tree
> The more he saw the less he spoke
> The less he spoke the more he heard
> Why can't we all be like that bird?

One evening about a week after Kelele arrived, Anna tried to release him, but again Morani's curiosity almost caused a disaster. Understandably many, many people, all involved in the sanctuary, wanted to witness the historic occasion of releasing another rhino into the sanctuary and made so much noise that Morani came to investigate.

Anna insisted that the procedure be stopped. This was going to end with a rhino getting stressed or injured, or a human getting hurt. She did not want to do anything to put rhinos, or humans, for that matter, at risk. Kelele's release would have to wait.

CHAPTER 17

Night Adventures

The very next evening, Anna returned to the boma. This time, only she, Karl, and Signadot, one of the rangers, were there. With no crowds, there was no noise. With no noise, there was no Morani. With no Morani there was no stress. Anna simply opened the gate and Kelele stepped out.

Only Karl, Signadot, and Anna were there to witness the addition of the sixth rhino on to the sanctuary.

That evening, under a full moon, Anna went on a night drive alone. A full moon made it easier for poachers to do their dirty work, which meant it was extra dangerous to be out after dark. Anna knew all this, and arranged for extra patrols on the sanctuary.

During the night, certain animals, and not just those that are considered nocturnal, were more active. Even rhinos often gathered and interacted more in the night than they did in the daylight. Anna was looking for rhinos, but also keeping an eye out for poachers.

She saw neither rhino nor poachers, but did spot her very first aardvark. "I do love it here," she wrote in her journal.

As a child, Anna had had some of her best adventures in the dark of the night, and she may have been somehow drawn to the night.

Once, when she was twelve, Anna tiptoed out of her silent, sleeping house. The village was in total blackout—with heavy blinds drawn and streetlights turned off—so as not to give the German bombers easy targets for their nightly raids.

She crept down the grassy hill toward the beach. The moon and stars reflecting off the water lighted her way. Her heart pounded, not so much from fear, but from excitement. She had finally convinced old Sydney, the gardener, to take her conger fishing. Sydney knew everything about fishing and thought the large conger eels were the best sport. Everyone knew you had to fish for them in the dark of night. Maybe they would catch a thumping great one that she could bring home and show her mum.

Anna spotted Sydney waiting by her little rowboat. She recognized his hat pulled low over his ears, his shoulders hunched. Definitely not a soldier. Anna and Sydney dragged the dinghy over the stony beach and into the river. Sydney took up the oars. All they had to do was slip over the submarine netting that blocked the mouth of the estuary and aim for the headland, the point of land where the old church sat.

It wasn't far. They could row there in hardly any time.

Once under way, Anna took deep breaths of the salty air. She often snuck out at night and had excellent night vision. The dark magnified the quiet, as did the lack of breeze. She knew the area was crawling with English soldiers patrolling the beaches to prevent a German attack. So, despite her feeling of contentment, every time the oars creaked, she strained her ears for the yell of a soldier from the shore.

But Anna never heard a soldier's yell. Instead, an enormous vessel broke the surface of the water, rising like a whale, right next to their tiny dinghy. Anna's heart clenched, Sydney grunted. Were these Germans, come to attack the Cornish coast? Would she and Sydney be captured, never to be heard from again? If she disappeared, her mum and dad would kill her. And what about Sydney? Anna regretted dragging him into her adventure. If only she'd stayed in bed this night, instead of gallivanting across the countryside, none of this would have happened.

"What the Bloody Hell do you think you're doing?" a very English voice called out from the submarine. Anna's heart unclenched a little bit. The soldiers were English, praise be, she thought to herself.

"We are only going congering," she called out. Perhaps if these men understood she and Sydney were innocents, not German enemies, they could continue their adventure.

Anna heard more cursing. The submarine pulled up next to her and strong arms grabbed and hoisted her and Sydney aboard. Stern-faced soldiers crowded around them, glowering. Anna's spirits sagged for a moment, but she quickly became fascinated by her surroundings. As the sailors led her to their captain she peered into the nooks and crannies of the submarine. Sydney, on the other hand, clutched his hat in both hands, slumped his shoulders and looked at his shoes as they walked the length of the vessel.

The captain was furious. "We could have killed you and it would have been your own fault. Are you nutters, taking this little girl out in the middle of the night?" He turned to Sydney.

Sydney just hung his head and said, "yessir," but Anna said, "Oh, don't worry about that, sir, it was all my idea. I made him."

Anna did not want Sydney to get in trouble. She knew full well it was all her fault. She had bullied Sydney into taking her. It had sounded like a grand adventure. The captain stared at Anna, his brow furrowed and his jaw muscles clenching and unclenching. Then, with a snort, he waved his hand and dismissed them into the care of some of the sailors.

"What will happen to my boat?" Anna asked.

The men scowled and one said, "We sank it, Miss. It's gone. And you're lucky we didn't sink it with you two in it."

The next morning, Anna and Sydney were put down at Falmouth Harbor, about five miles north of the estuary where their adventure began. The captain called Anna's parents to come get her.

As they walked down the ramp to the dock. Anna turned to wave to the sailors, her new friends. They all waved back. Sydney stared at her; his mouth opened and then snapped shut into a tight line. He stomped away, shaking his head and mumbling under his breath. Shortly after that Anna's father came to get her in the family car. He did not lecture her, but his stern demeanor and heavy silence made it clear he was deeply disappointed. That wounded her more than any yelling or lecture would have done.

After this, she was locked in her bedroom every night for a long time. But neither locks nor the disapproval of others could keep Anna from her adventures, day or night, as the rest of her life demonstrated.

CHAPTER 18

First Rhino Infant

Rebuilding the rhino population was a very slow-going, long-term project. Anna knew this from the start. Rhinos mature very slowly. Females don't have babies until they are six or seven years old and they are pregnant for more than one year (450 days) with each baby. Male rhinos don't mate until they are about nine years old.

Many years are spent raising each individual offspring. Female rhinos do not come into heat for at least three years after giving birth. Calves stay with their mother for at least those three years.

Rhinos typically stay with their mothers for three years. Here, a black rhino calf is almost as large as its mother.

A black rhino and her calf crossing a track on the sanctuary. All Rights Reserved for Rhinos, so trucks don't bother them. Mt. Kenya is in the far background.

So, when the sanctuary's population got a welcome boost with the arrival of three more rhinos—all of whom arrived pregnant—Anna and Ian were happy to receive them.

These three rhinos arrived several months after Rongai, Amboni, and Kelele. They came from Solio Ranch, which was founded in 1966 for cattle ranching. The owners, Courtland and Claude Parfet, fenced 13,000 acres of the property to protect the zebras, leopards, and gazelles that also roamed the land.

Throughout the 1970s and early 1980s, the Kenyan Wildlife Service brought more than a dozen rhinos to Solio, and some of those rhinos, in turn, had babies. The land has abundant acacia, fever trees, and shrubs to browse.

But the private ranch did not have as much security as Ngare Sergoi did. They had no around-the-clock, trained rangers. They had no electrified fencing or radios.

In addition, the ranch had too many rhinos. Anna and Ian were happy to receive the extra rhinos. Juno arrived in August. Anna, hoping the new rhino was indeed pregnant (it was very hard to tell if a rhino was pregnant), named her Juno for the Roman goddess of fertility. Juno was the largest rhino so far on the sanctuary.

Sure enough, six weeks after Juno arrived, Anna got word over the radio; Juno had a baby! Anna rushed to witness the miracle. She sat for two hours, "utterly entranced. It is so tiny and so adorable and I vowed it shall never know terror or pain from my species."

Ian and Tim joined her and watched in satisfaction and contentment. The calf lay next to its mother, its gray skin shimmering and its enormous ears overwhelming its tiny head. The humans jubilantly, but quietly, patted each other's backs. They watched as Juno tried to guide the infant to nurse. Their first baby! That night they drank champagne to toast this exciting new chapter.

"This does seem the culmination of all I have worked for," Anna wrote in her diary.

CHAPTER 19

Dismay

Their joy at the birth of their first rhino baby turned to dismay. Juno did not go near the baby after that first day. Her teats did not look large enough to have any milk in them. The baby cried and cried, which Anna quickly learned signaled serious distress. In addition, she saw that the mother had not discharged the afterbirth. Often, the release of the afterbirth triggers an animal's milk production.

It could be deadly if a horse didn't expel the afterbirth almost immediately but it wasn't a problem for cattle. Which was it for rhinos? Even the local vets didn't have the answers, since rhinos were not their usual patients. So many unknowns and so much worry.

Anna, Fuzz, and Ian decided they would focus on the problems they could manage. That included guarding against predators. Saturday night Fuzz slept near the baby to protect it from predators. He stayed awake most of the night, the stars a blanket above him. Predators stayed away, but so did the baby's mother.

At dawn on Sunday, Juno had wandered from the calf. Her afterbirth still protruded from her back end. Things were looking extremely grim. At noon, Peter, Dieter, and Ted came. The calf was still alive, but barely. They decided Anna would try to raise the infant.

Anna carried the baby, about the size of a full-grown German shepherd, home. She wrapped the baby in blankets and held it in her lap, trying to share her body heat. At her house, she wrapped the infant in more blankets and hot water bottles.

She fed it a little bit of milk, per (the veterinarian) Dieter's instructions, from a makeshift bottle. The infant struggled to respond, but it had very little energy. "The little sweetie with its blunt enchanting little nose only drank 400 ccs," Anna wrote.

Anna lay on the floor of the stable, holding the calf and trying to keep her warm. On Monday, just before dawn, the baby died in her arms. "My darling little rhino died. I feel utterly wretched," she wrote in her diary. She tried her hardest, and still the calf died.

Stumpy arrived soon after Juno. Although she had been crated at Solio the same day as Juno, Stumpy's arrival was delayed. Somehow in the course of the capture, she had fallen after she was darted and perhaps broken a bone in her foot. Plus she'd gotten her hips trapped between two iron bars of the crate, loosened her horn and injured her eye.

With her limp, her loose horn, injured eye and generally thin and poor condition, Stumpy looked especially feeble compared to Juno's magnificent form. Anna worried. If she was pregnant, Anna doubted her calf would survive.

Anna and Ian kept Stumpy in the holding boma for a couple of extra days to help her get over her travels, but while in the boma she absolutely refused to eat. So they decided to go ahead and release her, hoping that she would eat on her own. Stumpy found her friend, Juno, almost immediately and they gravitated to high, open ground, unlike most rhinos who liked to hide in the valleys. Once out of the boma, Stumpy settled right in.

Solia, the third pregnant rhino, arrived next. Her arrival at the sanctuary brought the number of rhinos to nine. Solia was a magnificent rhino, large, and well formed, with a dramatic, curving horn ending in a rapier-thin point. Although not as big as Juno, or Rongai for that matter, Solia had a domineering and high-strung personality. The three female rhinos, Juno, Stumpy, and Solia, tended to share the same territory, all three preferring the open areas to the valleys, just as Morani did.

Morani's time at the sanctuary proved to be temporary, sadly. Bull rhinos plagued him here as they had earlier in his life. Five months after he arrived, Godot attacked Morani and almost killed him. His gait was stiff and the trackers who observed him reported he could not urinate. Three days after the fight, Morani left his usual territory and hobbled to headquarters. He had been to headquarters maybe twice in his life, but perhaps he associated it with humans. He basically presented himself there in case the humans could help him. Morani let Anna lead him into a boma and clean and disinfect his wounds.

Given the extent of his wounds and how he moved, Morani must have been in a lot of pain, yet he let Anna tend to him without protest. Anna was amazed he didn't put up a fight. The next two days Fuzz gave him an antibiotic injection, and again Morani submitted to the process without a complaint. After two or three weeks it appeared that he had recovered. But Anna feared for his life and so, sadly, she lured him into a travel crate with some lucerne, and they drove gentle, sweet-natured Morani back to the orphanage in Nairobi.

CHAPTER 20

Keeping Up Spirits in Face of Setbacks

By the time 1984 had ended, Morani had been returned to Nairobi, Juno's calf had died, and Anna had to call a temporary halt to infrastructure building, such as building dams—to create watering holes—and roads. But there were some real accomplishments as well. When the year began, the sanctuary hadn't even been completed. Now there were eight rhinos on the property, and some of them were pregnant.

Now that the sanctuary had so many rhinos, Anna went "rhinoing," as she called it, every day. She typically went with Kinyanjui, one of the trackers who worked at the sanctuary.

Her goal was to lay eyes on each rhino daily. But this was no game park or glorified zoo. The rhinos were to feel completely free from humans. Free to live their lives in the wild.

Anna continually observed the rhinos and became convinced that much of the "received wisdom" about rhinos was incorrect. For example, one afternoon she went in search of Rongai because there was a concern that she had been pregnant and lost the baby. She found Rongai settled happily in the shade of a tree side by side with Amboni.

"Solitary animals my foot!" she wrote.

The trackers always made sure to stay upwind and out of sight of the rhinos. These were wild creatures, not pets. Despite her personal interactions with Godot and Shaba, Anna did not expect or want the rhinos to feel comfortable around humans.

Black rhinos have the reputation of being solitary, as in this photo, but Anna also often observed them hanging out together. Her observations also showed her that the conventional wisdom, that black rhinos were aggressive and belligerent, didn't appreciate that they were also inquisitive and intelligent.

In addition to protecting rhinos, the sanctuary protected every species within its fences. The black rhinos were a keystone species. That means, by protecting them, the sanctuary also provided a good habitat for many other species, from the rare Grevy's Zebra to the reclusive civet cat. The sanctuary also benefitted the people living nearby.

As the sanctuary became established, Anna understood that conservation efforts such as this only work if people living nearby benefited from them, as well as the animals. For that reason, among others, she always hired local people.

The sanctuary provided good jobs at twice the average pay. The locals valued that. Poachers were determined to get inside the sanctuary, and Anna was equally determined to keep them out. She stationed guards to patrol the perimeter. She also enlisted elite trackers who kept an eye on each rhino.

Listed as endangered on the Red List of Threatened Species, their populations have rebounded within the sanctuary. Lewa is home to about a quarter of the Grevy zebra population. These zebras, taller than the common zebra, have larger ears and narrower stripes.

The gerenuk, an antelope species, has an unusual feeding behavior. It stands on its rear legs to eat tall shrubs. Lewa Downs is one of the few places one can see the Grevy zebra, the gerenuk and the reticulated giraffe.

Reticulated giraffe

Meanwhile, Anna got the opportunity to go on another rhino-rescuing adventure in 1985.

She got word that there were a few rhinos living wild in the Mathews Range, a little to the north and east of Lewa. A mere ten or fifteen years earlier, a large population of rhinos wandered those hills, but poachers had slaughtered almost all of them.

Capturing a wild rhino was a complex and expensive operation, as Anna had learned with Shaba, but this rumor seemed solid. She decided it was worth spending the money to gather the team, including the helicopter and several trucks, to see if they could rescue another rhino.

In late January the team, including several trackers, Dieter the veterinarian, Ian's wife, Jane, and Ian, piled into several trucks—one large enough to carry a rhino if they got lucky enough to capture one—headed for the village of Wamba. They carried with them material and tools to build a temporary boma, as well as camping equipment and food for several days.

At Wamba, a tiny town in the hill area, they built a sturdy, temporary boma nearby. Then they made camp in a valley leading into the mountains.

The mountains were covered in a thick, cedar forest, with tall, straight trunks. But the rhinos weren't living in the gorgeous cedar forests. They made their home in harsh scrub at the foothills of the mountains. Anna and the others trekked through thorny bushes that grew so thick and tall they were forced to stoop and often crawl on their hands and knees to wind their way through the vegetation.

The day before Anna arrived, Ian had spotted a rhino but could not get close. Having at least glimpsed a rhino gave them hope that this expedition was not a waste of resources. The next day at dawn, Anna headed to a lookout spot high above the valley with a tracker named Errada. Errada was one of several local men living near Ngare Sergoi Anna hired as trackers. She became quite close to several, despite her weak Swahili and their weak English.

Anna struggled through the tough, tangled, and thorny thickets that scratched and bruised her legs. In addition to the difficult climbing, it started to rain, which is unusual in January. Then the temperature dropped. Anna and Errada got to their lookout spot. Without the body heat they generated from hiking, they shivered as they peered through the rain, looking for any sign of movement.

Perhaps, if Ian hadn't spotted the rhino the day before, they would have given up the hunt once their teeth started chattering, but knowing the rhino was somewhere nearby kept them at their post. Finally, Ian suggested they call it a day. Anna agreed.

She and the rest of the team slogged down the hill, back through the thorny thickets and returned to camp, wet and cold. Jane cooked hot food and made tea, which revived the team. Anna spent a damp night in her tiny tent.

The next morning, Anna found a dry shirt but had only her wet shoes and pants from the day before. Wearing damp clothes, she set out with Errada in the pre-dawn dark, sliding and stomping through the now muddy earth.

One bright spot in the dark misery was rhino tracks were deeper and easier to spot in the mud. Anna and Errada again hiked up high, watching for any movement in the valleys. At one point, a two-man team below them had trouble making sense of some fresh tracks, so Anna and Errada hiked down into the valley to help sort them out.

The four of them, with Errada in the lead, studied the tracks. Then they heard a noise. SNORT! Something was in the gully just below them. CRASH! The sound of breaking branches shattered the peace. An enormous creature of some kind was bashing around in the tangle of bushes. It was so close Anna forgot to breathe. This beast sounded bent on destruction the way it was charging around.

And then, before Anna could even think to be frightened, an enormous rhino erupted from the gully. Its tail stood up. Its ears were laid back. It ran as fast as it could away from the humans. Anna watched it go, amazed at how fast and graceful the rhino was.

Her heart pounded. She felt breathless. Such magnificence!

The team in the chopper also caught sight of the rhino as it galloped away, but they couldn't get a good shot with the tranquilizer gun because of the rough terrain. The last thing they wanted to do was sedate the rhino in an area where they could not then reach it with the truck.

It felt terrible to call it a day. They had come so close, almost too close in Anna's case. They had never before had a rhino in their sights and not captured it. They returned to camp, exhausted and dejected.

Anna, having had that close encounter thought the rhino had to be nearby.

Although she had been hiking up and down this exhausting terrain for eight hours, Anna went with Ian in the Super Cub airplane to see if they could spot it from the air. No luck. They returned to camp, and joined the others in another hearty, Jane-prepared dinner.

Then they collapsed into their beds, resting up to try again the next day. Their last day.

CHAPTER 21

Last Chance

Everyone was up early the next morning. Dieter had to be in Nairobi the following day and they couldn't safely capture a wild rhino without a vet on hand. Anna had spent a lot of money preparing for this capture, from building the boma to hiring the helicopter and some of the trackers from the KWS. Anna hated to imagine coming home empty handed.

Soon, Ian and several others spotted fresh tracks and off they went in pursuit, undaunted. The tracks were far apart and headed in a specific direction, so they knew the rhino felt disturbed and was moving quickly, not just ambling around.

Ian, who typically led the capture efforts, called Anna and Errada on the radio and asked them to climb down the ridge they were on—away from where they'd started their hike—cross the valley and go up the next ridge to look for the rhino. The thorny shrubs were so thick they couldn't find a trail through them.

About halfway down to the valley they came upon some very fresh rhino tracks. Perhaps the rhino had swung back around toward them.

Anna radioed to the others. Ian was skeptical because he, too, had found fresh tracks and he was in a different area. Ted and Tim hovered above Anna in the chopper to see what they could see and immediately radioed to her. *Anna, the rhino is right next to you, be very careful.*

The chopper was an essential tool in rhino rescue. But in this case, the chopper was a mixed blessing. On the one hand, the pilot was able to warn Anna and Errada that the rhino was nearby.

On the other hand, the chopper's presence, the thrumming of its engine and the shadows its blades cast on the ground, could scare or enrage the rhino—or both—and cause it to stampede right into the two people on the ground. Also, did Anna and Errada realize they were on the edge of a very steep cliff? Tim asked.

Anna was stuck in a thorny, very steep spot with an enormous, nervous rhino within spitting distance, not to mention being cold, wet, miserable, scared, and frustrated. But all she wrote in her journal was, "It was an interesting situation."

As terrifying and uncomfortable as this experience was, Anna had dreamed of this kind of adventure all during her childhood in England.

With a snort, the rhino charged off away from them, reducing the threat from that direction at least. The helicopter took off after it while Anna and Errada tried to make their way down from their precarious spot. Over and over Anna tumbled to the ground as she navigated the challenging terrain, only to end up on the far side of the mountain from their camp.

Meanwhile, the helicopter managed to get close enough to the rushing rhino to shoot a tranquilizer dart into its neck. It was not a female, as they had thought, but a magnificent, large, fat male with an enormous horn. He had tattered ears and a deep, nasty spear wound in his neck. Dieter treated the wound with disinfectant. He also checked the rhino's heart rate and breathing to make sure the sedative was not too much while the waited for the truck to come.

Tim, in the helicopter, meanwhile got the message to come rescue Anna and Errada.

"Bless him he came and whisked Errada and me over the mountain and deposited us beside the rhino," Anna wrote. After all that work, it would have been a shame to have missed the entire operation. Plus it saved them hours of extra walking.

Anna and Errada arrived in time to help hoist the rhino, tied to a sled, into the back of the truck. Although the distance to the boma was not too far, it took forty minutes over the rough terrain. Anna worried that the rhino would suffer from being tranquilized for so long.

They had yet to lose a rhino from being sedated too heavily or too long, but there was always a first time. In addition, the truck had no way to slowly lower the rhino onto the ground. They just slid the sled, with the rhino riding it, down a steep wooden ramp.

With a loud THUMP, the rhino and sled landed hard on the ground. Anna worried about the rough handling, though the rhino did not appear to suffer. Dieter injected the recovery drugs, Anna doused the rhino with water to help him recover, and soon the rhino staggered upright, looking "furious and magnificent!" As she often did, Anna named this rhino, Womba, for the area in which he was captured.

It was quite an adventure to get this rhino off the mountainside, but it was none too soon. "In the course of the expedition around the mountains we had come across the corpses of three dead rhinos—all with their horns chopped off and their faces horribly mutilated."

Still, Anna and the rest of the team could take some comfort and satisfaction in rescuing Womba, which gave them hope for the future of black rhinos.

CHAPTER 22

Samia

Shortly after capturing Womba, Solia gave birth to her first calf, the second rhino to be born on the preserve.

The day Solia gave birth, February 15, 1985, began like any other. Anna awoke with the dawn. She made her tea and sipped it while looking out her kitchen window.

Her eyes rested on the snow-covered Mt. Kenya far in the distance, and the dry and brittle vegetation just outside her window. They were in the midst of a major drought.

Karl was still sleeping when Anna called to her dogs and headed out for her daily walk.

Little did she know that her life was about to be transformed.

While feeding her horses, Anna heard on the radio that Solia had calved. She drove as fast as she could in her little yellow Suzuki to the spot where Solia had given birth.

Here, too, the vegetation was dried out, but Solia had found a safe place in the shade of a tall gum arabic tree, about one mile from the holding boma she had lived in when she had arrived.

Anna tried to be philosophical about whether the baby rhino would survive. After losing Juno's baby, which died in her arms, she didn't want to get her hopes up. They would see what they would see and only time would tell. But still she worried about the calf's odds of survival.

This part of Kenya sits almost on the equator, and it relies on two rainy seasons per year (a short one in November and December and a longer one mid-March until June). Without those rains, by February 1985, the landscape was parched. The rhinos were not getting enough to eat; was Solia healthy enough to have a robust baby, Anna wondered?

Anna allowed herself a moment of optimism. Maybe this baby would survive. It could happen, and if it did happen, that would be the very pinnacle of Anna's vision. What a thrill that would be.

Anna drove up and found Fuzz already there, crouched upwind in the tall, dry grass. Anna could not see any blood or sign of the afterbirth. Did that meant Solia had discharged the afterbirth and would soon produce milk? Solia's teats did not look full of milk and the calf was very small. Perhaps, because of the drought, Solia had not had enough nutrition to make milk.

Making sure to stay upwind of the pair, Anna crouched with Fuzz and Ian. She marveled, as she had with Juno's baby, at the sight of the baby's translucent gray ears just barely poking above the tall, brown grass. Otherwise the infant was virtually invisible; Anna could only spot the baby when its ears moved. The sight of such a tiny creature, which, if it survived, would grow to be an enormous beast, filled her with awe.

Solia wandered off several hundred yards to browse the nearby shrubs, dry as they were. The baby's cries were high pitched and birdlike. Solia ignored her. After their experience with Juno and her calf, Anna knew these sounds were a bad sign. When all was well, a rhino infant remains silent.

Anna mentally urged Solia to feed her baby, but she did not move a muscle. They wanted the mother and infant to feel as if they were alone. They hoped Solia would nurture and nuzzle the infant. They watched. They waited. Nothing. The only sound was the grunting of the Grevy's zebras grazing nearby and leaves and grasses rustling in the dry wind.

Night was coming. Anna and Ian debated. Ian wanted to leave some guards with the calf to protect against hyenas. Anna argued that was dangerous for the guard and the rhino. They arranged, in the end, for Kinyanjui to sit in a car with a spotlight.

Anna, meanwhile, slept on the top of a Land Rover at the nearby boma where Womba still remained.

Early the next morning, Anna and the trackers, Errada and Sygardal, checked the water hole. Solia had been there. Then they tracked her to where she was browsing, between the water hole and the infant. Throughout the day she gradually moved closer to the baby. Finally, at about three pm she lay down about twenty yards from the infant. That was as close as she'd been all day. That was as close as she ever got.

Anna dashed home to feed Karl and the livestock and then headed back. The baby had to be fed. But what to feed it? Anna did know that natural rhino milk was low in fat and protein and high in lactose and some trace minerals. But where would she get milk like this?

Anna turned to her veterinarian friend and colleague, Dieter Roche. Dieter recommended a mix of skim milk, non-fat milk, syrup, and vitamins. Anna promptly tracked down an enormous jug—the biggest baby bottle ever—fitted it with a nipple and filled it with Dieter's formula.

As the sun hung low in the sky, Anna coated her arm in Solia's dung, so she smelled like the baby's mother. She crept toward the baby. The infant screeched and fought but Anna managed to get two cups of milk into the little creature. "Getting well bitten in the process," she wrote.

That night Anna once again drove the Land Rover over to the nearby boma where Womba rested. She slept on the roof once again. Solia wandered around the truck all night. Anna lay awake, looking at the stars, and wondering what tomorrow might bring.

The next morning, Solia still had not approached her baby. Once again, Anna coated her arm in Solia's dung and fed the rhino calf. The rhino fought much less, mostly because she could barely lift her head.

CHAPTER 23

Kifaru Mama (Rhino Mama)

Finally, Ian convinced Anna to hand-raise the newborn.

"We were just starting to get into conservancy and every rhino was pure gold in terms of what it meant. It still is, but this was even purer gold," Ian Craig said of the event. "There weren't a lot of people who'd raised rhino calves . . . Anna had to pioneer and experiment herself in the whole rations, nutrition area."

That meant taking the baby to her own house. They did not make this decision lightly. Anna, in particular, knew that raising an orphaned animal is an all-consuming task. Rhinos nurse for three years. In addition, orphaned rhinos frequently died, whether from malnutrition, illness, or grief, it was hard to know. She remembered those feelings of heartbreak, remorse, and frustration when the first rhino calf had died in her arms. But she couldn't give up on this little treasure.

The decision having been made, Fuzz approached the weak, dehydrated baby. He crept toward it, speaking in a calm, quiet voice. "It's going to be okay, little one. We'll take care of you." He crouched down, just a few feet from the infant and the next thing he knew. WHOMP! The baby charged him, hitting him in his belly and knocking the air right out of him. Fuzz, gasping, picked up the brave rhino. She was tiny. Her umbilical cord was still attached. Fuzz carried her to the truck. Anna sat on an old mattress in the truck's bed, waiting to receive the calf.

Anna held the newborn calf in her arms, though it was about the size of a mini fridge. The wool of the blanket she had wrapped the baby in made her skin prickle and itch. She hummed and cooed to it as the truck bounced over the rutted paths. The mattress absorbed some of the shocks. Anna swayed her body to further smooth the ride for the "little one," as she often called the calf. The eighty-pound infant poked its wrinkled face out of the blanket. Then, with an exhausted squeak of alarm, it relaxed in Anna's arms. The calf was just too dehydrated and depleted to argue.

Meanwhile, in the back of the Land Rover, Anna's arms, although strong from riding and shoveling horse manure, ached and itched. The weight of the baby was making her legs fall asleep, but she did not loosen her embrace. Could she keep this treasure alive? What could she do differently from the first time?

The Jeep pulled up to the compound and Anna's house. Anna climbed out, brushed her short hair from her sweaty brow, grabbed a pitchfork, and made a soft, dry bed of grass in her stable for the rhino calf. The infant was cold to the touch, so Anna curled up in a blanket with the baby and used her own body heat to warm up the weakened creature.

Despite her exertions, Anna shivered in the cold night air. The rhino squeaked and squirmed. The stable smelled of horse and hay. The dust made Anna sneeze over and over again. She swatted at a swarm of mosquitoes circling her head, mercilessly biting.

Anna tried to snuggle with the rhino, but it was like cuddling a four-legged boulder. Anna's muscles and bones ached from lying on her makeshift bed. She fluffed the hay, but the ground remained rock hard. By midnight, she had had enough.

"That's it," Anna said, standing up. "It's got to be warmer and it will certainly be more comfortable inside." She picked up the infant and hauled her into the house, where they both snuggled on Anna's bed.

Luckily, Karl had just gone out of town and didn't have to come home to find a rhino in his bed . . . at least not this time.

Morning came after an endless, exhausting night, and Anna felt the tiniest bit of relief. This new calf had already survived longer than the only other rhino born on the preserve. But it was still dehydrated, undernourished, and chilled.

That first day, the calf drank many cupsful of milk, which pleased Anna. She was concerned that for all the eating the rhino did, she hadn't peed or pooped yet. Also, she worried that the rhino calf did not shiver, which was how mammals warm themselves. But Anna, always pragmatic, refused to let worry paralyze her. She would do her best and hope it was enough.

Anna offered a bottle to the calf, who was lying on the bed. She had to keep her fingers very near the rhino's mouth to keep the nipple on the bottle. That took a lot of trust, but the two had already bonded after yesterday's ride in the Land Rover. The infant was alone in the world, except for Anna..

"Luckily I find it easy to love baby animals," she once wrote. "You cannot pretend to them, for they sense it at once if you do not truly love them, and consequently, they cannot love you."

CHAPTER 24

Samia Struggles

Just three days after the "little one" was born, the rhino seemed better. "Dare I hope?" Anna wrote in her diary. That day, she decided to name the rhino Samia, a combination of Solia, the rhino's mother, and Sambo, her most beloved dog.

Two days later Samia even took a short walk with Anna and pooped a little, much to Anna's delight and relief. Samia happily slurped from her bottle up to five times a day.

As happy as Anna was about the rhino's appetite, the pooping situation worried her. When Samia pooped a week after she was born, it was a ghastly, foul-smelling diarrhea, not normal for a rhino of any age.

Still, Samia was eating, and that was something to be thankful for.

Anna led Samia on short walks, even when she was a few days old, so she could learn about her habitat. Anna was determined that Samia would return to the wild as soon as she could fend for herself. Anna had three years to teach Samia all she could about surviving in the wild. She would try to show her what to eat, where to poop, and how to interact with the other rhinos.

Raising a rhino was almost uncharted territory. Not many people had fostered a baby rhino. This was well before the Internet and information was hard find. Anna felt quite alone, but she had to try.

One day they went walking and stopped at a rocky outcropping. Samia sat on Anna's lap and chomped on a piece of grass. She was still under the weather, but she had spirit enough to enjoy the outing. Samia probably weighed about a hundred pounds, but Anna knew the calf needed the connection that came from sitting on her lap. As wiry as she was, Anna was able to hold the rhino's weight.

Samia matched Anna in toughness. Each time Anna thought Samia was going to die, the little rhino fought back. Her will to live might pull her through, Anna hoped. Every night Anna and Samia sat by the fire in Anna's house so Samia could warm up. The "little wee rhino," as Anna called her, happily guzzled her baby rhino formula, but her skin was still cold to the touch and she didn't shiver. Plus, her poops remained ghastly. Still, there were bright and entertaining moments, like the night the curious rhino gained some energy and climbed, first into Anna's lap, then on to the table, "causing a considerable crisis with the soup," Anna later recalled.

Imagine, having a rhino at your dinner table. And that was the least of Samia's adventures. But Anna, who could not have human children, indulged Samia and blanketed her with love.

Although Samia continued to have trouble with her digestion, Anna did not want to give Samia antibiotics. She feared that it would upset and possibly kill off the helpful bacteria in her gut.

What were her options? Anna wanted so much to save this creature she had become so attached to, but she had no idea what to do or who to turn to for advice. She continued to spend all her time with Samia, trying to keep her warm, fed, and hydrated; willing Samia to get better and to survive.

At ten days old, Samia was still was weak and could not get warm. In addition, her diarrhea was making messes all over Anna's house. Anna felt lost and alone, not to mention exhausted from the worry and from trying to sleep with a rhino in her bed.

Anna knew of one person in Kenya who had some experience with orphaned rhinos. Daphne Sheldrick, based in Kenya's Tsavo National Park with her husband, David, a wildlife expert, dedicated their lives to orphaned elephants. Daphne was born and raised in Kenya had also raised a few orphaned rhinos. She had identified a good milk formula for baby rhinos.

"Don't use that formula you've got," she told Anna. "It works better to use Lactogen," a commercial formula for human infants, and to change her diet in other ways as well. By this point, Anna had increased Samia's feedings from about thirty ounces per bottle to a little over forty ounces per bottle. Samia's appetite never waned, but her poops got stinkier and Anna's concerns grew.

Anna followed Daphne's advice, but Samia's poops got messier and messier. After a week on the new diet with no improvements, Anna was feeling frantic. She broke down and gave Samia an antibiotic. Even that did not appear to help right away. If anything, Samia's poops got smellier and runnier and her energy dropped. She lay on the floor in the stable, barely moving, not eating. Her diarrhea got so bad, she and Anna slept in the bathroom.

Anna became convinced that Samia would die and refused to leave Samia's side. Then she saw a kind of determination in Samia's eyes that made her a little more optimistic.

Karl returned from his trip and, despite his initial surprise, he went along with Anna's plan. Karl was used to Anna saving various orphaned animals. In the time they lived in Ghana, she'd rescued everything from an orphaned chimpanzee to an injured hawk.

One of Anna's biggest worries was Samia's inability to get warm. One day she tried tying a heavy rug around Samia like a horse blanket. She thought that would keep Samia warm enough that she could sleep on her own. Anna put Samia in the dining room and spent the night, at last, in her own bed, rhino-free.

The next morning Anna woke up and shuffled to the kitchen. On the way, she opened the door to the dining room and almost collapsed. Foul-smelling, rhino diarrhea covered the dining room carpet. The yellow excrement streaked every surface. Samia had rubbed her nose in the poop and scraped her feet through it, flinging it on the walls. Anna's dog, which had dashed into the room behind her, rolled in the fug. For the first time in all these terrible weeks since Samia was born, Anna wept. Was this her breaking point? Had her bottomless well of love for wild creatures dried up? How could she possibly go on? What human had the energy for this?

But for some reason, that day marked a turning point in Samia's health. Little bit by little bit, she got better. The next day Samia and Anna went for their customary walk and Samia had enough energy to play with some grass, give two little leaps and fall on "her precious nose." Then she walked around behind Anna and put her little round front feet on Anna's shoulders.

Just a few days later, Samia bucked and romped with vigor. Instead of their usual short walk, they spent the whole afternoon exploring the sanctuary. Anna allowed herself to imagine that perhaps Samia would survive. She could leave Samia with her blanket on in the stable for her afternoon naps, though, like many human infants, Samia would not fall asleep unless her mama, Anna, was there.

CHAPTER 25

Baby Bahati

As long as the sun shone and Samia ran around she was warm enough, but if she got wet or if the day became overcast, she got chilled. Even on sunny, warm days, Anna put Samia's big, thick horse blanket on her as soon as they got back from their walk and left it on until the next morning, when the day had warmed up.

Feeding Samia took gallons and gallons of formula. Here, Anna, feeds her with a makeshift baby bottle, a plastic jug with a nipple, which she held on with using her fingers.

After a few short weeks, Anna learned the meaning of many of Samia's vocalizations. For such a large animal, a rhino has a laughably high-pitched squeak. At first Anna didn't realize the sounds meant anything. But soon she recognized six different sounds: "'Eeeak' means 'where are you?' Another sort of 'eeeak' when waiting for her bottle means 'please hurry.' A loud 'eeeak' means 'I'm lost.' 'Huff-huff' means 'I'm coming.' A snort means 'what's that?' and the funny little noise which she makes when I put her rug on means 'you're troubling me.'"

Also, like a good mother, Anna recorded Samia's every benchmark. By the time she was one-month old, Samia had two sharp little teeth. In addition to her teeth, Samia's horn was poking through her leathery skin.

"I am getting a lot of bruises on my legs," Anna noted in her journal.

When Samia was about five weeks old, scrawny, mal-formed Stumpy had her baby. Although Anna knew Stumpy was probably pregnant, she imagined, given Stumpy's condition and the drought, that she would probably lose the baby or it would not survive if it was born. But much to Anna's surprise and delight, Stumpy's baby was healthy and fit. Despite being very thin, Stumpy nursed the calf, which Anna named Bahati, Swahili for "luck," and successfully raised Bahati into a large, strong rhino.

One week after Bahati was born, the rains came, which was a big relief. The next day Anna observed Stumpy and Bahati feeding together, when Bahati slid down a muddy bank. Bahati tried three times to climb back up the slope. After the third time, Stumpy stopped grazing, ambled down the bank at a much less steep spot, and led Bahati back up that way.

Although the rain was welcome, Anna worried about Bahati getting chilled. The weather had turned both wet and cold and Anna constantly wrapped Samia in blankets and brought her inside. Even so, Samia's skin often felt cold. How would Bahati fare out in the wild, far from indoor spaces and horse blankets?

But, to Anna's surprise and relief, Bahati did not suffer in the least from the weather. Bahati also appeared to eat far more thorny bushes than Samia ever did and his digestion never gave him trouble.

Perhaps the special mix of ingredients in his mother's milk helped Bahati stay warm and also gave him a good, strong digestive system. Bahati grew far bigger than Samia, even though his mother was so tiny and ill formed. After Stumpy weaned Bahati, when he was about three and a half, she finally started to fatten up. Before that, all her nutrition seemed to be dedicated to her calf.

CHAPTER 26

Sabatchi

That spring of 1985, as Anna devoted herself to the months-old Samia, rhinos continued to arrive on the sanctuary. With almost a dozen rhinos now on the property, she felt optimistic that this sanctuary would really succeed.

In April, Anna participated in another rhino rescue, this time from an area near Ololokwe, a massive, flat-topped mountain, or massif, that rises straight out of a valley. Ololokwe is home to the Samburu tribe, who herd cattle and goats. The Samburu consider Ololokwe sacred and they co-exist peacefully with the wildlife, including rhinos.

Two years earlier, in 1983, when Anna and Karl had first arrived at Ngare Sergoi and were building their house, Anna went with Ian to investigate reports of five rhinos living on the massif. They hiked all day for two days through the thick forests and dense bushes and up and down steep inclines. They saw many, many rhino tracks, but the rhinos hid very effectively in the leafy vegetation.

Anna and Ian were of two minds about moving the rhinos away from Ololokwe—if they ever found them. Of course, they would love to have them safe in Ngare Sergoi. But perhaps they were better off staying put. As their own experience showed, the rhinos were very good at hiding in the thick vegetation. They talked about creating a small sanctuary there.

It was a perfect location; the rhinos could thrive there if they had the proper protection. They talked of armed guards, and even of building an airstrip at the top of the mountain, but Anna could not afford to fund that project. They were talking with other organizations that were interested in helping with the funding when they got word, in 1985, that poachers had moved in and slaughtered every rhino on the mountainside.

Again and again, just as Anna felt that they were making progress in stabilizing and maybe even growing the rhino population, poachers came in and murdered every rhino. And for what? Just money. For money they were prepared to wipe this amazing creature off the face of the earth.

It was like the dodo all over again.

In the spring of 1985, Anna and the others headed to Ololokwe to see if there were any survivors, for they'd heard of a single rhino that had come off the mountain and was wandering in the plains. They found an immature female in very poor condition. This surprised Anna because there had been a lot of rain that month and the vegetation was lush.

Perhaps the stress of losing her mother at such a young age, not to mention the rest of her family group, caused the rhino, which they eventually named Sabatchi (another name the mountain is known by) such stress that she never completely recovered. Perhaps that stress also made her more susceptible to infection.

Sabatchi, a three-quarter ton young adult female, attached herself to Fuzz. She never left the compound where Fuzz lived and worked. The door to his actual house was not very strong and "she'd often just push her way through the door . . . When I woke up in the morning and came out of my bedroom I'd find her lying in the sitting room," Fuzz said.

Fuzz just walked around her. Often she'd lie against the door to Fuzz's office. Luckily, the door was a Dutch door, meaning the top half opened while the bottom half was closed (and the other way around). That meant when Fuzz needed to leave his office all he had to do was open the top half and "crawl out over her."

"She was awesome," he said. "You just couldn't leave the porcelain out . . . I felt more comfortable around Sabatchi than I did Samia."

Photo courtesy of Lewa Downs.

Fuzz Dyer in 2001.

CHAPTER 27

Clever Rhino, March & April 1985

Fuzz may have preferred Sabatchi, but Anna doted on Samia. She took Samia walking every single day. That way Samia could learn the terrain of her home. She learned the smells of the buffalo, the giraffes, and the other rhinos. She learned the sounds of the wind in the grass, the call of the weaver birds, and the grunts of the Grevy zebras. She learned the feel of the ground under her feet, the slopes and flat plains, and the dusty dry ground and the lush wet areas. Anna did all this so that Samia learned that this was her home.

Anna often climbed over rocks on their walks. In response, Samia huffed in a way that said to her, "I'm worried" or "help me." Anna did not help Samia but encouraged her. By June, Samia clambered over rocks with much less anxiety. Samia also liked to play with rocks, moving them using her nose and sprouting horn.

If Anna came across poop from another rhino, she scuffed it. She hoped by demonstrating this behavior, Samia learned how to do it also. Anna realized, after the way Samia had kicked her poop all over the dining room, she knew to do this instinctively.

Instead of scuffing the poop, as Anna did, Samia often ate some of it. Samia ate a lot of animal poop, whether it was rhino, zebra, or even cow. It might have seemed disgusting, but Anna did not stop Samia. She felt strongly that she should never discipline Samia, but help her grow in as natural a setting as possible, despite being fostered by a human. In addition, her friend Dieter, the veterinarian, said that Samia would know best what she needed. Perhaps by eating all this dung, Samia was getting some bacteria into her intestine that would help her make better poops.

After a few months, Samia's intestines seemed to improve. Her poops did not look like Bahati's, but they were not as loose as they had been. Samia still struggled to stay warm. When Anna compared Samia's health to Bahati's it became clear that Bahati, being raised by his mother, had better intestinal health and was better able to handle temperature changes.

Still, Anna continued to do her best, confident—most of the time—that Samia's energetic nature would help her adjust eventually.

Anna tried to show Samia what to eat. She pulled the branches of the various types of acacia and other shrubs toward her own mouth. *Yum Yum!* she said to Samia, hoping it looked to Samia as if she was eating the branches. Samia watched her and sometimes mimicked her, but she never did enjoy the thorny acacia.

Black rhinos, with their prehensile upper lip that enables them to grasp things the way an elephant does with its trunk, are typically browsers and eat small shrubs more than grass. White rhinos, with their wide mouths, graze more like horses and cows, eating only grass.

As much as Anna encouraged Samia to wander the preserve, when night came Anna locked Samia into the heavily reinforced stable. It was dangerous for her out in the sanctuary with no mother to protect her from the other adult, especially male, rhinos.

Every evening Anna lured Samia into the stable by putting lucerne, a sweet alfalfa, and some other yummy food in her stall. One time Anna forgot the lucerne, which was one of Samia's favorite foods. After that mistake Samia's checked every evening to make sure she had received her treats before she let Anna leave.

Anna making sure Samia gets her lucerne

Three weeks later, Anna conducted an experiment. She purposefully did not leave the lucerne with Samia's nightly rations. Samia inspected the pile and proceeded to tell Anna "in no uncertain way that the lucerne was missing." Anna loved that she could understand Samia's vocalizations. Samia's cleverness pleased her immensely.

Gradually Samia got stronger and stronger. But for every win, there was a heartbreak.

That spring Anna got word that two rhinos had been poached in other sanctuaries.

"I can't bear it," she wrote.

Samia had been born in February, during a drought. By the time she was two months old, the rains had returned and the sanctuary sprang back to life. When Anna took Samia walking there were many more plants to show the little rhino.

A researcher who studied the range of plants black rhinos feed on found thirty-eight at Ngare Sergoi alone.

Samia still had a lot to learn about her environment, but she was a good student. One day when Anna and Samia walked together, they came upon a herd of cows. Samia panicked, fled, and tumbled down a hill.

The next time they met with cattle, Samia held her ground. She stood close to Anna, and she gave some anxious huffs, but she did not run. Samia was quite a clever rhino.

CHAPTER 28

Audience with the Pope

Meanwhile, the word had gotten out about Samia, the little "wee rhino." Many, many visitors came. David Craig often brought them. He knew many more people than Anna because he had grown up on this very land and his family had lived in Kenya for several generations. Anna, on the other hand, was an outsider. She was new to the area. She was new to rhino conservation. And she was new to Kenya. People tend to be skeptical of outsiders.

Anna enjoyed meeting people, though she had little patience for those who were stuck up or self-important. Still, Anna appreciated the donations some people gave to the sanctuary. In April alone she spent about $14,000 of her own money. Many nights she tossed and turned, worrying about how to pay for everything the sanctuary needed. She wrote about selling her jewelry and at one point even considered selling the bulldozer and the Super Cub airplane she had bought for the sanctuary.

In July, when Samia was five months old, something happened that upset Anna—and Samia—very much. Someone in Nairobi who heard the good news about Anna raising the abandoned rhino decided that Samia was just the special attraction they should share with the Pope, John Paul II, who was scheduled to visit Kenya.

This was all well and good if the Pope wanted to come to Ngare Sergoi, but no, that was not the plan. The organizers of the Pope's visit insisted that Samia travel to meet him. To Anna this was ludicrous. To shove a still-not-one-hundred-percent-healthy baby rhino into a crate and fly her—all two-hundred-and-fifty pounds of her—halfway across Kenya to a lodge on the west side of the country, just for the entertainment of humans, was preposterous. It also reflected that these people who held Samia's fate in their hands did not care one whit about her welfare.

Anna had absolutely no power. There was no one she could appeal to. She felt like Samia was hers: she was raising Samia; spending every minute of every day with her; teaching her how to be a proper rhino, to the best of her ability. But in truth, Samia was the property of the Kenyan people, just as all of Kenya's wildlife was, and as such Samia was at the beck and call of the government. Anna had to accept the situation. Her only recourse was to make the trip as stress free as possible for the little, precious rhino she'd bonded so deeply with.

This was all about impressing the Pope, the big cheese. Anna hated big cheeses. Big cheeses in her mind were people filled with self-importance, people who had no sense of humor and certainly couldn't laugh at themselves. She loved what she called "little cheeses," people who were humble and worked hard and were interesting and made her laugh.

Anna hated pomp and ceremony and hierarchy. Consequently, she was not impressed by the fact that this effort was being made on behalf of the Pope, even though Pope John Paul II was a very popular and much-loved figure. And that was not to say she wouldn't have enjoyed Pope John Paul II if she'd had a chance to meet him. Maybe he was a funny, self-deprecating kind of guy. But she didn't have the chance to find out because she was not allowed to accompany Samia, being "the wrong sex, race, and nationality." Instead, Kiptamoi, who Anna described as her gardener, accompanied Samia to meet the Pope. Anna felt deeply bitter and outraged at the blatant unfairness of the situation. Neither she nor Samia had any say in this decision, which impacted the two of them the most.

CHAPTER 29

Samia Takes a Trip

For the trip to visit the Pope, they built a traveling crate and Anna trained Samia to go into it by putting food in it. They also built a small boma, or pen, so she could get used to being confined. And then, with Dieter's help, they experimented to find the right dose of a tranquilizer so Samia could travel in relative comfort.

Traveling by truck was stressful enough for a rhino. Anna could only imagine how Samia would react to flying. Unfortunately, their first tranquilizer attempt backfired. Instead of calming her down, the first dose drove her crazy and she charged first Dieter, then Fuzz, and finally Kiptamoi, the man who was going to take care of Samia during her Pope visit. They tried a second type of tranquilizer, which worked fine. That put Anna's mind at ease on at least one aspect of Samia's trip.

And now Samia's schedule turned completely upside down. Instead of being free to roam all day and closed into the stable only at night, Samia remained penned up virtually all day, mostly in the boma but for many hours also in the crate.

Animals of all kinds do best with a routine, a schedule. Anna attempted to create this new schedule for Samia so by the time she traveled it would be her new reality.

Everyone also wore white robes around her so when she saw the Pope in his full-length white robe, she would not be startled. No one wanted Samia charging the Pope or his assistants.

Anna knew this new routine was not ideal for her little rhino. She feared very much for Samia's health. It had only been a month since she began to believe Samia might survive. And now, being crated for hours per day when she was used to having the run of the sanctuary was making Samia very ornery and stressed out.

Samia hated it. She showed her feelings by "knock(ing) both the crate and the boma to bits." Anna felt terrible about how upsetting all this was for Samia, though she also was a little impressed by how strong Samia had grown, despite her insides still being upset.

Finally the day came for Samia to make her journey. At dawn Anna gave Samia half her bottle of rhino formula. Two hours later she fed Samia the other half in her crate. The crate was then loaded onto the back of a pickup truck. Anna and Kiptamoi climbed in also. They sat on either side of the crate, trying to keep Samia calm. They hoped by being next to her, Samia would feel less stressed.

They drove to the little airstrip near the sanctuary without incident. Samia would fly in a small propeller plane with the seats removed. In addition to Samia, Anna, and Kiptamoi, veterinarian Paul Sayers and a photographer squeezed into the little plane. Even with Anna in the plane trying to calm her, and a small dose of tranquilizer, Samia was distraught. She wailed and plunged back and forth in her crate.

Their extremely experienced bush pilot, Fiona Alexander, had difficulty taking off with a charging rhino in the hold of the plane. Fiona was not sure such a heavily loaded plane could fly over the Mau Escarpment, so she took a longer route around it instead of over it.

Finally, they landed at the Keekorok airstrip in the Masai Mara reserve. Samia had suffered on the trip; she'd bashed about in the crate so much she'd bloodied her nose and become overheated. Now she was dehydrated and constipated. Anna was supposed to fly back to Nairobi at this point, but she refused to leave until Samia had pooped.

Samia ate and drank and peed, but she did not poop. The last commercial plane to Nairobi left. Anna refused to leave. Instead, she booked herself into a room at the resort. The next morning Samia still had not pooped. If Samia could smell some rhino poop it would help her, Anna knew. Anna asked for permission to take Samia on a walk to find rhino poop.

She was told there were no rhinos in the area anymore. Well, zebra poop would do, she said. Anna got permission but was told, stay near the road because there were lions about.

Anna and Samia set out to find some poop. They walked along the road and at every pile of zebra droppings Anna got down on all fours. She sniffed and scraped the droppings. Would Samia get the message and poop? They ambled along, each time Anna showing Samia the zebra poop. Soon they had several minibuses following along, watching the crazy antics of this small woman and this large rhino.

Finally, after two hours, Samia pooped. Success!! Anna scooped it up in a plastic bag and brought it back with her to the boma. With this she could establish Samia's toilet. Now her job was done, and she had to leave Samia to the people managing the Pope's event. With a sore heart and a guilty conscience, she left Samia and returned to the sanctuary.

The Pope's visit included a tour of the wildlife on the Masai Mara, where he saw giraffes, a cheetah, and some elephants. He also met Samia and he gave her a pat. Their interaction lasted less than a minute. And yet, Samia was gone from home for six full days. At last Anna got the green light that Samia could return home. "Here we are, Samia," Anna said when she arrived by Samia's side. "Huff huff huff, puff," Samia replied. It was as if Samia wanted to tell Anna everything that had happened since they had parted.

Anna traveled with Dieter in a larger plane to take Samia home.

The return flight was uneventful. Both Samia and Anna were happy to be home. Samia had lost weight in the course of her travels, but Anna thought Samia could recover once they returned to their proper daily routine.

They took lots of walks through the grasses and shrubs and along the ravine near Anna's house. Anna continued to pretend to eat acacia thorns and scuff at rhino poop. Samia continued to explore her environment, running back to Anna whenever she got startled by something unexpected.

CHAPTER 30

Gentle (and Clever) Giant

After her return, Samia acted less independent than before her trip. She squeaked and cried when Anna left her. She did not wander as far from Anna during their walks like she used to.

One night shortly after her return, Samia's blanket slipped off. She cried and cried until Anna came to the stable from her house and readjusted the blanket. Anna took some comfort from the fact that Samia could, at least, now communicate with her when something wasn't right.

Even if Samia had experienced some anxiety after her trip, she was as smart as ever. One day, while Anna was in the kitchen mixing Samia's bottle, Samia used her prehensile lip to open the latch of the gate. She ambled into the kitchen. Anna scooted her out.

A few minutes later, Samia again opened the latch and headed into the kitchen. Anna escorted her out and returned to the kitchen. Samia did it again. Again Anna shepherded her out.

Samia liked this game. Samia never tried to knock the gate over. Every time she carefully lifted the latch. Finally, Anna parked her truck in front of the gate. The game was over . . . for now.

Samia did enjoy "playing" with Anna's truck. Often Anna would come out of the house to find that Samia had butted the door, or climbed on the hood, crushing it. When this happened, Anna called Fuzz. "Um, can you come have a look at my Suzuki?" she asked.

Photo courtesy of Naomi Campbell

Anna often drove around in her little yellow Suzuki truck to check on the rhinos scattered across the sanctuary. Samia also used it as a playmate.

Fuzz would find the back door taken off or some new collection of dents. Samia once "wrote her name" with her horn on a visitor's car door. But Samia especially liked playing with Anna's little yellow Suzuki. It drove Fuzz crazy.

"Samia caused lots of strife, unless you are her mother, then it's all pleasure," he said. "Samia would butt a car and all Anna would do is tap her nose with a stalk of grass and say, 'don't do that.'" Finally, Fuzz arranged to build a cage for Anna's car. Though sometimes, when Anna went to park it, Samia would be standing in the cage.

Just a month after she'd returned from her trip to the Pope, Samia was summoned to the annual agricultural show in Nairobi. This time Anna had no advance notice. The very next morning after the summons, a truck arrived to take Samia away. At least she didn't have to fly again. However, no one had counted on the fact that Samia had grown so much in the last month she could no longer fit into her Pope cage.

Quickly, another crate was built and Samia walked right in. Anna felt like a traitor, knowing what was ahead. Samia wailed and cried when the lorry drove away with her in the back. Anna, once again, was ordered to stay at home.

At the show, Samia was kept in her crate almost all day. Visitors came to see her, to feed her a little alfalfa. A member of the KWS stood guard. Six days later, Samia returned. Now she coughed and her nose dripped. Samia dragged herself out of the cage. Anna, frustrated and furious, set about once again nursing her baby back to health.

Anna felt like she was the only one who truly cared about Samia's well being. These faceless, nameless people who demanded Samia's presence at these large occasions had no appreciation for the individual creature. It was all about show for them, and Anna resented that deeply.

CHAPTER 31

Clever Rhino

Despite Anna's worries about Samia's health the little rhino was growing bigger and stronger. By the middle of October Anna and Samia walked between two and three hours per day. Their walks took them all over the sanctuary with Samia spending much of the time eating.

One day three giraffes glided from around some thorn bushes and lowered their heads to investigate. Their large, long-lashed eyes took in the sight of a human, a large black dog (Sambo), and a small rhino walking together.

Samia looked up from a bush she was browsing and came face to face with these strange, new creatures. She snorted in alarm and ran between Anna's legs.

However, the "wee rhino" was now so large that she knocked Anna right over. Since she could not hide behind Anna, Samia sat on her, "huffing and puffing her consternation."

October and the rains came. At first no rain fell on the sanctuary but the glare of the sun was broken by glorious clouds, and finally Anna relaxed for the first time in months. "Oh it's so lovely on the eyes!" she said of the clouds. A few days later just a few drops of rain fell but it was enough for Samia to snort and dance around.

Samia continued to demonstrate how clever she was. In November, Anna had some low voltage wire installed so that Samia would not mess with the garden fence. Samia burned her nose on it several times. Anna turned the knob to lower the setting as Samia watched her.

After that, Samia stood on a rock and unhooked the wire with her horn. Anna replaced the wire connection. In five minutes Samia unhooked it again. Point for Samia.

Because their eyesight is so weak, rhinos rely more on their sense of smell. Being the good rhino mother that she was, Anna wanted Samia to practice using smell. One day she devised a lesson. She hid up the road.

When Samia called out for Anna, Anna remained hidden. Anna hoped Samia would track her using her sense of smell. Instead Samia opened the gate and let the dogs out. She then followed the dogs, who found Anna. That cannot have been instinctual, Anna mused. That is one smart rhino.

As she grew, Samia also became more agile. Instead of worried and scared squeaks when faced by steep or rocky terrain, Samia clambered right over the obstacles. By the spring, when she was a year old, she could climb up the steep bank from the ravine near Anna's house faster than Anna.

One day, needing a bit of help, Anna grabbed Samia's tail as Samia headed up the hill. After just five times of Anna doing this, Samia stuck her tail out horizontally to Anna any time they went up a hill. What a fast learner Samia was.

On the other hand, Samia still resisted eating thorny acacia. Anna kept trying to show her to eat acacia, since it was a regular part of rhino diets. She pulled the branches toward her and made munching movements with her mouth, smacking her lips. "Yum, acacia," she said to Samia.

Perhaps Samia could tell Anna was just going through the motions because she never ate much of the thorny shrub as a youngster. She preferred softer grasses and shrubs.

When she did eat acacia, "she had her lips pulled back and a really comic expression on her face as she tried to manipulate the thorns." Perhaps other rhino mamas could show their babies how to eat the thorn without impaling themselves—and Bahati certainly ate acacia without concern for the thorns—but Anna never figured out the secret.

Anna continued to feed Samia in the stable at night. There Samia received her sweet alfalfa and horse nuts, which was a kind of horse food in pellet form. Samia loved the treats but she never pushed or prodded Anna to get at them.

Photo courtesy of Naomi Campbell

A young Samia near the stables where she spent the night as a youngster. Visitors, such as those in the background, often came to marvel at the little rhino.

"She is one of the very few young animals I have ever had who never pushes or demands food roughly," Anna wrote. "She stands by my side and asks for it. Even if I get delayed talking to someone, she just continues to ask, never pushes. She is never rough except in play or when afraid."

One time, Anna gave Samia horse nuts and then walked away. Samia let out a kind of trumpet noise Anna had never heard before. It was as if Samia were torn between her beloved horse nuts and going with Anna, because when Anna returned, Samia stopped trumpeting.

CHAPTER 32

Samia Grows Up

By the time Samia was eighteen months old, Anna was confident she would survive. Her poops became less runny. As she got bigger she was also able to keep herself warm by shivering. Managing her body temperature had been Anna's biggest worry.

No matter how much she loved Samia and doted on her, Anna never lost sight of the ultimate goal: for Samia to live in the wild like every other rhino on the preserve. Keeping herself warm was essential to that goal.

At this point, Anna's money worries inspired her to experiment with a different, less-expensive formula. But that formula, a calf formula rather than a human baby formula, gave Samia terrible diarrhea.

For everything Samia had gone through before this; her abandonment at birth, her struggles to stay warm, her trip to the Pope and then to the agricultural fair, it was this change in formula that appeared to lay her low. The light went out of her eyes. She hardly had energy to lift her head. It took two harrowing weeks for her to recover.

That was the last time Anna experimented on Samia's digestion. Perhaps Samia's stomach would always be sensitive. Perhaps she would always struggle with catching a chill. But once again she romped. She walked with Anna and Sambo, Anna's favorite dog. Her eyes were bright, her ears perked. She appeared to be thriving.

One day Samia leaned against a barricade and accidentally knocked it down. There was no doubt, this "little wee rhino" was growing up. Samia seemed to sense her growing size. When she wanted Anna to swat flies off her and Anna was sitting down, Samia did not walk across Anna's legs as she used to when she was small. Instead she walked around her.

Samia tried to be gentle, but sometimes she could still be awkward, especially when it rained. After a rain, the ground became sticky and slick, like a thick pudding, bringing out Samia's frisky and silly side. One time after a rain, Samia rolled her eyes and romped around so exuberantly that she accidently knocked Anna down three times.

Each time, Anna got up and brushed herself off before Samia crashed into her again. Anna, frustrated, swatted her on the nose with a blade of grass. Samia then spun in circles around Anna, who stayed splayed on the ground. The young rhino became so dizzy she fell down too, with legs sprawled out.

Samia tried to control herself, but rain was just too exciting. She rollicked and squelched in the mud, rolling her eyes. The chances of her accidentally hurting Anna, who was in her fifties by then, or Sambo increased so much that Anna stopped walking with Samia when it rained.

As silly as she got in the rain, Samia could tell when Anna felt poorly. Once a horse reared and fell on Anna and she was in pain for several days. Samia sat quietly with Anna and did not try to play or cavort with her. Likewise, when Anna had malaria, Samia sat by her side, but did not try to play.

CHAPTER 33

Other Rhinos

At about eighteen months old, Samia was almost four feet tall at her shoulder and her feet were each eight inches in diameter; roughly the size of a personal pan pizza. Samia was growing bigger and more robust, though she was nowhere near full grown.

As Samia grew larger her relationship with Anna changed. She went from hiding behind Anna when scared or startled to putting herself between Anna and the danger.

One day on their walk they came upon the sanctuary's one white rhino, Makora. Anna stopped to wave him away as Samia continued on home. Instead of continuing or hiding behind Anna's legs, Samia stepped toward Makora, as if to protect Anna.

"How brave Samia is to try to take on a rhino at least sixteen times her own size," Anna wrote.

Luckily, Makora stopped following them, and Anna and Samia were able to trot home.

Once Samia was eighteen months, Anna knew she had to familiarize her with the other ten rhinos, and vice versa. But how to do that without putting both Anna and Samia in danger?

Even though Anna had come to appreciate and admire rhinos and to see the ones at Ngare Sergoi as individuals— not mindless brutes—she also appreciated that rhinos were very large and very strong and very fast. They were generally nervous and could hurt a human, and a young rhino, without even trying.

To further complicate efforts for Samia to join the other rhinos, Samia instinctively feared them. Anna assumed Samia had, at least in part, picked up on her own fear. Anna had a healthy respect for the wild rhinos and made sure not to get too close. Samia, perhaps, picked up on Anna's own feelings.

Still, there were unexpected meetings. One day, when Samia had turned one year old, Anna, Sambo, and Samia were returning home from a tromp in the bush. Anna, in the lead, came around a tree and almost ran into Juno, a full-grown female black rhino.

They were practically nose to nose.

Anna snorted her best rhino snort of alarm and then she ran. She ran with a pounding heart and gasping breaths. Samia took off after her, but, in a move right out of a slapstick movie, managed to scoop Anna up on her back. The two charged through the bush until Samia ran under a "wait a bit" thorn bush. Anna fell off. Her eyeglasses went flying. Her false teeth fell right out of her mouth.

Anna groped around frantically in the undergrowth, found her glasses, and, with an exhalation of relief, perched them on her nose. Now she could at least see. Then she hunted for her teeth.

Once she found them, she made sure that Juno posed no threat. Juno was just as alarmed as Anna and her companions, but she had not charged them. She simply stood nearby huffing and snorting.

Anna calmed Samia and Sambo down as best she could and they headed home. What a shame it would have been to get trampled by one of the very creatures she devoted her heart and her pocketbook to.

Remembering that close call, Anna decided the safest way to introduce the rhinos to Samia and the other way around was by simply spending time in the sanctuary, which they had been doing since Samia had first come home with Anna. By the time she was eighteen months, Samia scuffed, ate, or pooped on the other rhinos' droppings, which helped her become familiar with them, at least from a distance. In addition, Samia communicated occasionally with the other rhinos by puffing and huffing in a particular pattern.

One day, Rongai and Kelele made the distinctive "who are you" puffing sounds from across the valley and Samia responded. Anna had to take comfort in that long-distance interaction and hope it would be enough when the time came for Samia to live full time with the other rhinos.

As she grew older, Samia paid more and more attention to the other rhinos on the sanctuary. And they paid more attention to her. Generally speaking, this was a good thing. It suggested that Samia would be successfully incorporated into the rhino population.

The only rhino Anna really worried about was Godot. The huge, bull rhino could be violent and he began to take an interest in Samia. Anna didn't know why he started to come around the house, since Samia was still a baby in rhino terms, but she was quite sure Godot would "bash up" Samia if given the chance.

Rhinos have few predators, other than humans, but they often kill one another in fights. One way to reduce that risk is to provide a lot of space. Lewa Downs was 5,000 acres, which should have been plenty of space, but Godot could not be dissuaded from hanging around the house.

Anna strengthened Samia's boma to protect her in case Godot's interest grew. Samia not only "helped" by filling the post holes in with her horn, but she also ate a hose, "yet again," as Anna wrote.

Anna's instincts about Godot were right. Shortly after the barricade was strengthened, Godot knocked down a nearby tree and tried to knock down Samia's boma. Anna prayed the boma would withstand his assaults.

Another time Godot was hanging by the house, near the chicken coops, when Samia was out on her own. Fuzz and Anna drove over to where Samia was and enticed her to follow Fuzz's truck, which Samia did quite happily. They managed to get Samia safely into the stable without Godot being any the wiser.

Godot's antics did not change Anna and Samia's daily routine of walking for hours through the sanctuary. Anna encouraged Samia to explore on her own, but she never missed her daily walk with Anna. In fact, she could be jealous of anyone who tried to join them.

The problem was, especially because of Godot, they often had to have a tracker with a gun escort them. When one of the trackers, like Orogai, or even when Karl or others that Samia knew perfectly well, joined them—whether to act as a lookout for Godot or just for the pleasure of their company—Samia behaved poorly. One time she even chased Orogai up a tree.

Anna might have thought Samia was a sweetheart, but she was still a rhino and could inflict injury if she wasn't careful.

CHAPTER 34

Money Woes

The sanctuary was not open to the public at this point, but visitors came often to the sanctuary to see and meet Samia. Typically they were government officials, or friends of Anna or the Craigs.

One time the British High Commissioner came for a visit. Samia picked him up with her horn. Anna was mortified, but the commissioner was very pleased. He understood the gesture of affection right away, Anna wrote in her journal.

In 1987, when Samia was two years old, several staff members from the Kansas City Zoo visited Ngare Sergoi for the first time. Anna hosted them for lunch on the verandah of her home. Anna's verandah was perfectly placed to look out over the lush palm trees, bamboo, and rushes growing in the valley and hear the gurgle of the mountain stream that ran through it. Beyond that was open savannah and on the horizon Mt. Kenya rose to the heavens.

When it came to talking about Samia and the sanctuary, Anna could be charming, engaging and, of course, passionate. The zookeepers were so amazed and impressed by all that Anna and everyone had achieved that when they got home, they worked to get support for Anna and her rhinos, eventually raising more than $600,000 per year, through their national organization, American Association of Zoo Keepers (AAZK) and the "Bowling for Rhinos" program. This relationship continues to this day.

These kinds of visits rarely paid off to quite that degree, but they occurred often. Samia almost always cooperated, which Anna appreciated. Samia's comfort in both the human and wild world was helpful to Anna's fundraising efforts, and yet Anna worried. Could Samia become fully integrated within the rhino community if she kept coming back to Anna's house?

Anna and Samia

Photo courtesy of Naomi Campbell

Samia appeared to provide the answer . . . By the time she was almost three years old, Samia often spent much of the day away from the house. She occasionally would be gone all day. Anna knew this was good. But like a mother whose teen gets their driver's license and is gone for hours, that didn't keep her from worrying. She was always relieved when Samia came galloping home at dinnertime.

Meanwhile, Ian and his family had agreed to double the size of the sanctuary, from 5,000 acres to 10,000. They needed money for eleven more miles of fencing. Anna's money, no matter how she tried to reduce costs, would not be enough to continue to run the sanctuary.

The fund raising from AAZK, among other groups would prove to be critical to the sanctuary's continued success.

Meanwhile, Samia continued to show her cleverness.

When Samia was two and a half years old, Anna agreed to let visitors photograph her giving Samia her evening bottle outside the stable. But after her bottle, Samia refused to go in the stable. Anna gave up, figuring she would get Samia inside later.

Anna went to take a bath. She was in the tub when she heard the bedroom door open. "Who's there?" she called out.

"Whoo Whoo Whoo," came the reply.

Samia came right into the bathroom. She put her enormous front feet on the edge of the tub. She might have joined Anna in the bath, if Anna had not quickly leaped out.

Samia had lifted the latch of the gate using her prehensile lip as a finger and walked right into the house.

CHAPTER 35

Samia Leaves home

Samia was not only clever, but growing in strength, often to Anna's surprise. One day Samia took a mud bath in the overflow from the water tank. Then, feeling playful, she lifted the tank lid with her horn and banged it up and down. The lid was so heavy it took six men to budge it.

Like any parent who looks up one day and is surprised their baby is all grown up, Anna marveled that this big, strong healthy animal was the same creature she carried home in her arms and who she nursed back from the brink of death time and again.

On her third birthday, which fell on the day after Valentine's Day, Samia ate Anna's hat. "Not exactly what I had in mind for a rhino birthday cake," Anna wrote. Shortly after that, Samia broke a barricade again and wandered into the garden. From there she headed for the kitchen looking for Anna and got stuck in the doorway between the kitchen and the dining room.

Rhinos cannot turn their head to look over their shoulder. When something surprises them from behind they jump around, reversing their direction. The few times Samia reversed direction while walking with Anna she knocked Anna right over. This move inside the house would create chaos.

Happily, Samia seemed to understand. She stood still as her little tail whisked back and forth and her ears swiveled. Thinking quickly, Anna grabbed a gallon jug of cooking oil from the counter. She poured it all over Samia's hide and rubbed it to coat her gnarled, tough skin. Anna then gently backed Samia out of the doorway. Samia meekly followed Anna to the stable where Anna locked her in until Samia's dinner was ready.

In the spring of 1988, Anna got permission to move Godot to a different sanctuary. He had caused so much turmoil within Ngare Sergoi that he was putting the entire project at risk. He had fought with Morani, Sabatchi and Womba and badly injured them all. Womba had died of the injuries Godot inflicted. Anna didn't think rhinos would fight themselves into extinction, but she didn't want to test that theory. By April, they had moved Godot into a boma. Soon he was gone, moved to a different sanctuary. Anna and Samia could walk Ngare Sergoi in peace now.

After Samia got stuck in the doorway, Anna knew the time had come. Samia was big enough to live on her own, especially since the threat of Godot had been removed. In addition, Karl's health had been failing for the last year. Anna had traveled with him back and forth to Nairobi for all kinds of testing. Then Karl was hospitalized in Nanyuki, which was closer but still an hour drive away. She tried to visit him regularly, but it was very hard. Especially when the rains came.

"Sometimes the road becomes impassable as there has been torrential storms upon the mountain so sometimes we are completely cut off," she wrote to her god daughter, Naomi Campbell, a nurse who lived in England. "Last Saturday it took me 3.5 hours each way instead of the usual 1.5 and even my strong nerves have got a bit tattered!"

Still, Anna appreciated the effect of the rain on her world at the sanctuary.

"We've now had a total of eight inches of rain," Anna wrote to Naomi that spring. "More than twice what we had in the whole of last year. Our world is lush and green and beautiful with flowers and the period of death is over and all animals start to put on condition [get healthier and are well fed] and birds rush around with mouthfuls of housing materials."

Karl's health had deteriorated so much that Anna could no longer take care of him and the facilities at Nanyuki were no longer sufficient for his needs. She made arrangements for Karl to live in a nursing home in his native Switzerland. She never considered moving to Switzerland. She could not leave her beloved, adopted homeland. Not to mention Samia. Ultimately, she had to choose between her husband and, essentially, her child. She chose her child.

Anna planned to leave in mid-May to get Karl settled and situated in his new home. Samia had to be completely weaned and capable of surviving entirely on her own by that time. That meant no more bottles of formula or alfalfa and horse nuts.

In April, shortly after Godot had been moved to another sanctuary, Samia spent her first night outside the stable. Even with Godot gone, Anna sat in bed with her eyes wide open all night. She lay there, a cattle prod and a rake by her bed, and listened to Samia's cries. Samia ran up and down along the fence outside Anna's house calling and calling. Anna could tell that Samia was outraged rather than afraid, but if the tone of her cries changed, Anna could charge to the rescue.

The next morning Samia greeted Anna with such relief. The next night she only wailed until midnight. Perhaps she wandered off at that point. At dawn, she happily greeted Anna at the gate. On the third night Samia did not complain at all. However, in the morning she appeared worn out. Like Anna, she did not get much sleep.

Over the first week it became clear that the weaning process stressed Samia. She became a little chilled and thin. When they took a walk together, Samia tried very hard to sit on Anna's lap, but Anna refused. By Anna's calculation, Samia now weighed more than three-quarters of a ton, or 1,500 pounds.

After ten days, Samia was totally weaned. Her ears were cold and she had a runny nose, but she had "a lot of bounce." Anna was determined not to do anything unless Samia became much worse. Anna knew that Bahati, the calf that was born shortly after Samia and raised by his mother, was not yet weaned, but Anna had a different timetable because she had to leave soon for Switzerland.

By May it had rained so much that the drift became a real river. Anna waded across. Samia trumpeted and cried from the opposite bank. When Anna ignored her, Samia waded in. She discovered playing in the river was as fun as rolling and sliding in the mud.

In the middle of May Anna left to take Karl to Switzerland. She was gone for two weeks. In all that time, Samia never came near the house.

CHAPTER 36

Anna Comes Home

As soon as Anna got home from Switzerland, the tracker Orogai took her to where Samia liked to rest (a few km south of the house). They approached to about a hundred feet away from Samia. Anna quietly called her name. Samia emitted a loud snort. She jumped to her feet and charged full speed toward Anna. Her ears were back. She was "huff huff"ing in greeting.

Anna crouched down. Just before she reached her, Samia suddenly stopped running and pressed her face into Anna's. Anna held her nose between her hands and returned her greeting.

Samia smelled Anna all over. When Anna got up to get in the car, Samia followed. She galloped behind the car all the way back to the house. Samia stayed near the house until Anna came out for her evening walk, which they took together. At dusk, Samia wandered off.

Samia had lost a lot of weight while Anna was gone, but she acted fine. Anna was determined that Samia manage on her own from here on. Samia continued to join Anna every day when she took her walk, and the trackers reported that Samia had spent time with several of the other female rhinos. All in all, things were looking good.

By October, however, Anna broke her vow. It had become very dry again and she could not resist supplementing Samia's diet with alfalfa and horse nuts. Still, Samia's spirits seemed good. No matter where she was on the sanctuary, she came to join Anna daily for her walks. Often Anna could hear Samia's greeting, *huff huff,* before she saw her.

One day she heard Samia coming. The wind was blowing from Samia toward Anna so she could not have smelled Anna on the wind. When Samia came into view, she was trotting along with her nose to the ground. This was the first time Anna saw Samia actively tracking her. She was pleased.

Protecting rhinos is an emotional roller coaster; for every success there are many tragedies. In November all the rhinos at a nearby park, Meru, were slaughtered by poachers. Anna went to a meeting where they discussed whether to de-horn rhinos in order to protect them, an idea she was strongly against.

Later, Anna took a walk with Samia and told her about the idea. "To my surprise she rolled her eyes wickedly and then proceeded to give me a lengthy demonstration of just what a little rhino can do with her horn if she really tries," Anna wrote. "Oh, to have had a video camera with me."

Samia turned four years old in February, 1989, the year after Anna took Karl to Switzerland. "She is big, in lovely condition and very beautiful," Anna wrote in her journal. A few months later she had to put down her beloved dog, Sambo, who was eighteen years old. Sambo had been Samia's steady companion since her birth. And, of course, she was something of a namesake to Sambo, since "Samia" was a combination of Sambo and Solia.

Although Samia only came by the house every other day or so, she stayed by the house all night the day Sambo died. The next day she also stayed by the house. When they took their walk, Samia showed no interest in playing in the mud and water even though she never missed an opportunity before. Here was yet another indication that Samia and Anna communicated on a deep, wordless level.

That year Samia performed in a commercial filmed at the sanctuary. Anna was happy that Samia earned some much-needed money for the sanctuary and a little proud that

Samia behaved perfectly. Soon after, famed animal behaviorist Desmond Morris came to the sanctuary to make a documentary about Anna's efforts, and particularly about Samia.

CHAPTER 37

Capture of Kikwar

In 1990, the team got word of a wild rhino in the northeast part of the Matthews Range. Opportunities to rescue the last few wild rhinos were few and far between. A large group headed there and set up camp. The area was gorgeous and green. The Matthews Range, covered in trees, towered above them. The plains around them were covered in flowers and waist-high grasses. Butterflies flitted everywhere.

Still, the beauty of the area did not reduce the increasing activity of poachers. To do this rescue now was extremely dangerous and everyone was on alert.

"It was a hairy time in Kenya," Will Craig remembered. "There were lots of shifta (poachers). They would shoot at your car."

Fortunately, the team was large and there was some safety in numbers.

Anna and the team were up at dawn on Friday. All the beautiful and sweet-smelling flowers hid thousands of burrs, making walking tough going.

"I felt like a hedgehog who has had his skin put on inside out," she wrote. "Even worse were the cutting vines that lurked in the grass and lacerated our legs so badly that each step became a pain. As my legs became bloodier I tried to think of flowers and butterflies and rhinos, but as the hours passed such positive thinking became increasingly difficult."

The group looked everywhere. They found plenty of elephant, lion, and hyena tracks, but no rhino. The rhino did not seem to want to be captured. It made sense that it was hard to track, since it had survived on its own for so long.

At dinner after that first wet day, the group heard that a local farmer had found fresh spoor. They went to bed optimistic, but rain during the night washed away any potential tracks. Anna woke up tired and damp. They continued to hunt on foot day after day, often soaked by heavy rainstorms. Anna got a stomach bug and was bedridden one full day. The group finally spotted the rhino, but it was too late in the day to capture it.

The next day Anna got up. Though she felt weak, she would not miss out on the capture.

Anna walked with the trackers, slowly moving east for almost three hours through the bush and brambles. For as long as she spent in the bush, she never developed a tracker's eye. She felt deep admiration and awe for these men—they were always men—who could read the ground like a book. One of the trackers grabbed her and jumped to the side. Not a second later the rhino they'd been tracking erupted from the brush and ran, bashing through the growth like a boulder.

The helicopter, piloted by Tim, herded the rhino toward a more open area. Dieter darted the charging bull from the air and it went down.

As Anna watched Tim guide the helicopter, Ian yelled, "get up that tree." Luckily there was one Anna could clamber up. Just then, three elephants came charging through, evidently disturbed by the helicopter. They rushed on when Ian yelled and waved his arms. Then Anna and Ian jumped down and followed the group to the riverbed, where the rhino had gone down.

And there he was, a "lovely, fat male maybe 7 or 8 years old," Anna wrote. They named him Kikwar, after the area in which he was found. On the rollercoaster of life at Lewa, this was certainly a high point.

So far so good, but the transfer of Kikwar to the conservancy proved particularly challenging. First, they had no sledge or way for Kikwar to get into the crate they'd prepared. So, while Kikwar lay, still sedated, in the riverbed, they led a rope from his nose to the front of the cage and then through the other side. Dieter gave the male rhino enough of the recovery drug that he staggered to his feet, at which point, every person hauled on that rope and the rhino walked into the cage.

Once the rhino was loaded Tim whisked Anna off in his helicopter and gave her a ride home. Anna marveled at the beauty of the landscape, which was particularly striking from this vantage point. Tim deposited her by Fuzz's house at five pm, well ahead of the rhino caravan. In the process of exiting the helicopter she fell right out. Fuzz had to pick her up off the ground. For all her determination, nothing could change Anna's clumsiness.

Kikwar and the rhino caravan arrived at the sanctuary at ten pm, and it took another three hours to unload the crate. Because the rhino had to be loaded back end first (and unloaded front end first), he spent all that time tipped nose down and mashing his face into the end of the cage. The poor bull had lost his horn and gotten a bloody nose. Despite the rough journey, Fuzz released Kikwar to the wild one week later, and he was soon seen browsing throughout the sanctuary.

CHAPTER 38

Rollercoaster

Life on Lewa, like the rainfall, was a continual rollercoaster of joy and grief, of satisfaction and frustration, and of peace and strife and worry. That would never change. Anna had set for herself and the others a daunting task. It was not surprising that things did not always go smoothly.

But sometimes things did go well.

Anna's work and the sanctuary also began to get some international recognition. The United Nations recognized Anna's work with a United Nations Environmental Protection Global 500 award.

In addition, *National Geographic* came to visit with Anna and Samia. The magazine was doing a special issue on private conservation in sub-Saharan countries. Anna was very pleased with the photos they took of her and Samia.

Another special about the sanctuary and Samia had aired on ABC in prime time. All this publicity felt like a real accomplishment. The more they got the word out about their efforts, the more hope they had for donations.

Things were going well within the rhino population as well.

Samia turned five years old. While not quite full grown, Samia was now a full-fledged member of the rhino community. That spring another rhino joined their group. Osupat was a large male brought from Solio Ranch, like Solia, Stumpy, and Juno. Although Osupat did not like people and would charge cars, Anna noted that he was gentler toward the female rhinos than many male rhinos she had observed.

Shortly after he arrived, Anna saw that he and Samia were spending a lot of time together. Anna was so happy that they were a couple.

"Osupat is so gentle with his womenfolk!" Anna wrote.

Meanwhile, the team got word of another wild rhino, the last on a heavily forested and very steep mountainous region east of Lewa Downs. Both Lewa and the KWS had paid guards to try to protect the rhino. They went in January to try to capture the rhino but had no luck. A few months later, it was poached, its bloody carcass left to rot in the sun.

At the sanctuary, there were also some very hard losses.

Osupat, together with Kikwar, fell to their deaths in the midst of a fight; and Rongai seemed to have overbalanced while grazing near an edge and fell to her death as well.

Drought did not help matters. For the entire calendar year of 1991, the sanctuary had almost no rain. In addition to the drought, the air was fouled by a volcano in the Philippines and the oil rigs fighters had set on fire in the course of the Gulf War, when Iraq invaded Kuwait.

Between the droughts and rhino accidents, by the end of that year the sanctuary had lost six rhinos and had only one born, this to Samia's mother, Solia. Solia was a very good mother to this baby, which Anna named Zamia.

Still, the entire group at Ngare Sergoi was striving forward: plans were afoot to not just double the sanctuary, but grow it by a factor of six, incorporating all of the Craigs' land, known as Lewa Downs, as well as the government-owned Ngare Ndare Forest Reserve to the south.

Anna was becoming less involved in these plans; as a non-native Kenyan, she didn't have the clout to lead this project. In addition, she was very happy tending to her horses and dogs and rhinoing on the land near her home.

Photograph by Boyd Norton

Anna took daily walks with her dogs and Samia.

If they could raise the money for the miles of fencing they would need, the sanctuary would grow from 10,000 acres to more than 60,000 acres. By 1993, the entire enterprise became known as Lewa Downs Conservancy, in recognition of its growth and expanded goal of conservancy throughout northern Kenya.

Those conservation efforts included making sure the local communities benefited from the sanctuary's activities. Lewa Downs helped fund local schools and launch several local businesses. Again, Anna's heart was all for the rhinos, though she appreciated these other efforts and understood their importance.

CHAPTER 39

The Last Rhino Rescue

There was just one more wild rhino the group knew about, and they set about to capture it in January of 1993. They traveled to the north of Lewa Downs. Somali shifta (poachers) to the north were very active and so they had to undertake the operation swiftly. This rhino, Kenu, was a "small but powerfully built rhino with no ears, probably caused by a near miss with spotted hyena when he was a baby." This was the last wild rhino Anna's group would capture and bring to Lewa Downs.

Kenu was a wild and aggressive bull rhino who became Samia's mate. Not the best match, as far as Anna was concerned. Where Osupat was gentle, Kenu was violent, not just toward humans, but toward his own kind. Anna could understand how he came to hate humans, considering how many wished to kill him, but his violence toward rhinos was on a scale she'd never seen. Many times Samia had to intervene between Kenu and various humans, especially Anna.

One time while Anna was taking a morning walk Samia came to greet her. Suddenly Kenu erupted from the bush, charging toward Anna. Samia planted herself between Anna and Kenu. That enabled Anna to return home safely. Another morning Anna came out of her house to greet Samia without seeing Kenu standing nearby. Again he charged. Again Samia jumped between him and Anna. Then for forty minutes Samia "breathed an intricate pattern of sounds that clearly controlled him." After this stretch of time, Samia moved off, and Kenu followed her.

Samia had completely transitioned from the protected to the protector.

With her long, sharp front horn, a full-grown Samia presents a magnificent appearance.

Samia protected Anna from other threats, too. One time, Anna was late coming home from her evening walk. She did not like to be out at dusk, since that was one time of day animals were the most active. As she hurried along the track, Samia joined her right before she came upon three white rhinos, each almost twice Samia's size. Samia snorted, laid back her ears, and trotted toward them in an aggressive manner. The rhinos, "obviously astonished" by her behavior, moved off into the bush. Samia returned to Anna and walked with her home. She then rubbed her nose against Anna and returned to the bush.

Samia also protected other members of the staff and even guests, whom she had never met, against other rhinos, including her mate. Samia seemed to always understand her special role as a kind of ambassador between humans and rhinos.

Anna and Samia had a remarkable relationship that changed from Anna as the protector to Samia as Anna's protector. No matter how long Samia lived in the wild with the other rhinos, she always came back to Anna's to check in with her.

The 1993 drought finally broke in October, when the sanctuary got six inches of rain. That was a big relief because, although Anna supplemented several of the black rhinos' diets with lucerne and horse pellets, the other animals on the sanctuary, particularly the buffalo, waterbuck, eland, and warthogs, suffered terribly. By then the sanctuary was home to fifty-three black rhinos, thirty-seven white rhinos, as well as numerous, rare Grevy's zebras, reticulated giraffes, and more.

CHAPTER 40

A Marvelous, Miraculous Surprise

The happiest day of Anna's life started out unremarkably. Samia had not been seen for a couple days but that was not unusual. Still, trackers kept an eye out for her.

Anna had no cause to worry and was going about her business, doing chores at her house and observing Shaba and her well-grown male calf, who were on the hillside nearby. Suddenly Kenu showed up, spoiling for a fight. He attacked the male calf. Shaba fought back. Dirt and dust flew. Grunts and roars sounded as the two large beasts collided. Anna called for help over the radio and jumped into her Land Rover, intending to separate them. She figured her vehicle was fairly rhino proof. But she never got a chance to try because her truck got stuck on rocks and shrubs. Fuzz came in the sanctuary's Super Cub airplane to dive bomb the fighting rhinos.

In the midst of this chaos Anna got a call over the radio that trackers had found Samia. She was just to the north of Anna's house and she had a baby with her.

Leaving Fuzz to deal with Kenu and Shaba, Anna went with Joseph, another of the trackers, to observe the little miracle. She crept through the bush to where she could see Samia munching on browse. There, in the long grass nearby, Anna saw two tiny gray ears. The baby was not crying. Anna knew that was a good sign. She watched some more. The baby got up and wobbled toward Samia. It nosed around Samia's belly. Samia stopped eating and stood quietly. The baby nursed. It was clear Samia had plenty of milk. Then the baby lay back down. Samia laid her enormous body down next to his tiny one. What a marvelous rhino mother Samia was.

Anna felt so much joy and deep, deep satisfaction. She was a rhino granny. She never would have imagined, all those years ago when she carried little Samia in her arms back to her own house, that this day would ever come. This had been her dream; her vision. To have a place black rhinos could breed in peace and restore their numbers. Somehow this particular infant, this infant of her "rhino daughter," brought it all into sharp focus: She had achieved her ridiculous, impossible plan. Here was her own sweet Samia, her "little wee rhino," with her own infant.

Anna felt plenty of worry mixed in with the overwhelming joy. She was not at all certain that Samia, having been hand-raised, would know what to make of a baby. Could a human-fostered rhino care for her own offspring? Here was the culmination of her grand experiment. What would be the result?

That first night Anna worried so much she could barely sleep. Would Samia know that animals that posed no threat to her could injure or even kill her infant? Would she know to watch out for the lions and leopards that roamed the sanctuary? A herd of elephants had just passed through. Would Samia know to guard against them?

As the days passed, Anna saw again and again that Samia was an exemplary rhino mother. That eased her worry, though the feeling that replaced it was bittersweet. This was the moment, Anna knew, her bond with Samia would break. Rhino mothers are extremely protective of their babies. They are quite solitary during the entire first year of their baby's life. Anna knew if she approached Samia, Samia would most likely charge her. So the sign of true and total success would be, with the arrival of this calf, Samia would leave Anna.

For three days Anna contentedly observed Samia, always being careful to remain out of sight. But on that third day, everything changed. Absorbed in watching the pair, neither the tracker nor Anna noticed the wind shift. Before they realized, the breeze carried their scent to Samia. Samia lifted her nose. She pricked her ears. Samia came straight toward where Anna hid.

Anna knew she should retreat, but her knees were shaking so hard, she just sat down instead. Samia, together with little Samuel—as Anna had named this infant—came to Anna. There was Samuel, so small, with such glossy, smooth, soft skin.

It made Anna think back to the days, a decade ago, when Samia was just his size. Samia laid her enormous head on Anna's lap. Anna petted her and cooed over her, just as if she were a little puppy. Even a baby would not break the bond between her and Samia.

After that, every morning Samia and Samuel came to the garden gate to greet Anna. Samia would huff and breathe her greeting to Anna. Samuel would squeak his little rhino calf sounds. Anna imagined Samia knew she worried about how they fared. Anna was sure Samia came every morning to reassure her all was well. Anna made sure not to touch Samuel, but Samuel learned to accept her scent nevertheless.

One morning Samia came to greet Anna, but Samuel was nowhere in sight. Anna's heart plummeted. She instantly panicked. Where was the calf? Had something terrible befallen him? Just then, Samuel woke up from beneath a nearby bush and squeaked like a little whale. Samia rushed to his side, accidentally knocking Anna down. Anna stayed sitting as she watched Samia gather up her calf. Samia returned to find Anna on the ground, so, as she had done for so many years, she turned around and offered Anna her tail.

Friends for life.

Samia and baby Samuel walking away after a visit with Anna and her dogs.

AUTHOR'S NOTE

"Oh this crazy life I have chosen freely," Anna wrote. "Of dust, of danger, of death, of loneliness, of no family, few friends, only my love for animals and only their love for me. It is enough. I am filled with love, joy, acceptance, and surely as I go along I shall find the courage and strength that I need from those that I love: rhinos, dogs, dust, thorns, my world. My beautiful world."

The sanctuary has not only continued, but thrived, and all because of Anna's crazy dream, the Craig family's buying into that dream, and Anna and Samia's unlikely relationship.

That first year of the sanctuary, about a dozen black rhinos lived there. By the time Samuel was born, the sanctuary held five times that number. Today, Lewa Downs, holds approximately 10 percent of Kenya's black rhino population. Not only that, but the area of protected land has grown from 5,000 acres to 61,000 acres. The sanctuary also protects many other species beyond the black rhino. It has become a refuge for elephants, leopards, and lions but also smaller, more elusive animals, like the civet and the sitatunga.

In addition, Ian Craig and others have worked to create the Northern Rangelands Trust, a network of other communities throughout the region of Kenya north and west of Nairobi, that also are protected environments, as well as safe corridors so that animals can travel from Mt. Kenya south. Lewa Downs is at the heart of the Rangelands Trust.

The Trust is also about helping the human members of these communities, not just the animals. By helping establish schools and small businesses, the Trust encourages the residents to see the protected animals as a source of revenue rather than a nuisance. School children visit Lewa Downs regularly so that they can learn to value and appreciate the native animals of their country and see how they can enjoy and protect them.

When researching Anna's remarkable life and the singular relationship she had with Samia, it broke my heart to learn that both she and Samuel died in 1996, as the result of falling from a forty-foot cliff.

More even than when Karl died, more than when any of a number of her close friends died, this loss was unbearable. The daily reminders of her life and adventures with Samia and Samuel were too painful. Shortly after Samia and Samuel died, Anna moved to South Africa to retire far from her beloved sanctuary. She lived there, on the edge of another sanctuary, with a dozen dogs. She left much of her heart behind.

Still, without Anna's intervention, Samia would have died as an infant. Anna understood, even in those early days, that even when the price of love is loss and grief, it is worth it. Together, Anna and Samia brought so much attention to the plight of the black rhino and to the sanctuary efforts. Samia put a real, lovable, and sometimes comical, face on the black rhino, an animal that had suffered bad PR.

Although Anna moved away, she continued to support the sanctuary every way she could. She visited for long periods of time. She continued to raise funds for the sanctuary and to travel. But she never lived full time at Lewa Downs again.

Anna died in 2013, almost twenty years after Samia's death. She willed all her money to Lewa Downs. She called it the Samia Trust.

Acknowledgements

As with any project that requires research and travel, I am indebted to many people, but I will give a special thank you to Naomi Campbell (no, not THAT Naomi Campbell), Anna Merz's god daughter who opened many doors for me and got me started on my journey. Patty Pearthree and her connections to the AAZK (American Association of Zoo Keepers), who made it possible to travel to Lewa Downs with AAZK and shared her memories of Anna and Samia, and to the countless people who read and reflected on my/Anna's story, with special thanks to Susan Santiago, Elaine Bearden, Linda Skeers and, as always, my husband, Ben Williams.

I would also like to note that the books Anna herself wrote were invaluable and all quotes that didn't come from my own research came from what Anna herself wrote.

Resources

Organizations that Help Protect Rhinos

• **Lewa Wildlife Conservancy**. The sanctuary that Anna Merz co-founded. http://www.lewa.org
• **Save the Rhino**. This non-profit works to protect rhinos, reduce illegal horn trade, involve local communities and bring experts together. http://www.savetherhino.org
• **Northern Rangelands Trust**. A network of community conservancies in the northern and coastal areas of Kenya and Uganda established by Ian Craig. https://www.nrt-kenya.org
• **Tusk**. Working for the last 30 years to advance and support conservation across Africa. http://www.tusk.org
• **Rhino Resource Center**. Supports research and conservation of rhinos worldwide. http://rhinoresourcecenter.com

Books by Anna Merz

• *Rhino On the Brink of Extinction*. HarperCollins, 1991.
• *Golden Dunes and Desert Mountains*. African Medical Research Foundation, 1992.

Deb Aronson is the former assistant regional adviser of the Illinois chapter of the Society of Children's Book Writers and Illustrators (SCBWI) and has been a member since 2008. Her true story of the famous filly who beat all the boys *Alexandra the Great: The Record-Breaking Filly Who Ruled the Racetrack* was published by Chicago Review Press and she has published several articles (all non-fiction) in the children's magazines *Muse* and *Ask*. She loves to write nonfiction stories about ordinary people (usually women) doing extraordinary things; stories she wish she'd had in middle school.

CPSIA information can be obtained
at www.ICGtesting.com
Printed in the USA
LVHW101538300623
751168LV00039B/401

9 781960 373045